19.64

HAUNTEI
BRITAIN

Also by Derek Acorah:

The Psychic Adventures of Derek Acorah
Ghost Hunting with Derek Acorah

DEREK ACORAH

HAUNTED BRITAIN

OVER 100 OF THE UK'S
SCARIEST PLACES TO VISIT

HarperElement
An Imprint of HarperCollins*Publishers*
77–85 Fulham Palace Road
Hammersmith, London W6 8JB

The website address is: www.thorsonselement.com

and *HarperElement* are trademarks of
HarperCollins*Publishers* Limited

Published by HarperElement 2006

1

© Derek Acorah 2006

Derek Acorah asserts the moral right to be
identified as the author of this work

A catalogue record for this book is
available from the British Library

ISBN-13   978-0-00-722067-0
ISBN-10   0-00-722067-7

Printed and bound in Great Britain by
Clays Ltd, St Ives plc

To Ray and Jayne
for their endless support

CONTENTS

ACKNOWLEDGEMENTS

I would like to thank everybody at HarperElement and LIVINGtv and all the people who have helped over the past 12 months.

INTRODUCTION

'All houses wherein men have lived and died
are haunted houses!'
Longfellow

Following the tremendous success of *Ghost Hunting with Derek Acorah*, I was inundated with requested to compile a book of locations throughout Britain that are reputed to be haunted – and I was certainly spoiled for choice.

One of the most difficult things when deciding to go on an investigation into the paranormal is finding the right location. Hopefully *Haunted Britain* will take the hard work out of this by suggesting over 100 of the most haunted places in England, Wales, Scotland and Northern Ireland, divided into areas for ease of reference. No matter where you live or how little you are prepared to travel, there will always be somewhere worthy of a visit if you are on the hunt for a ghost or two.

While I have not yet been able to visit all the places covered in this book, I very much hope to investigate them in the future. Some of these sites may be slightly off the beaten track, but I'm sure all are worthy of the ghosthunter's attention.

When undertaking an investigation into the paranormal it is as well to remember that there are many different types of ghostly manifestation. First, there are the 'feelings' we all pick up from atmospheres. When entering premises, take care to note in which room or rooms you feel comfortable and in which you feel less at ease. Use your basic psychic senses – we all have them – to assist you in the first steps of your investigation by picking up on the residual energies left in a property by previous occupants. Obviously unless you are a trained medium you will not be able to experience specifics, but you should be able to identify areas where you feel there is more likelihood of paranormal activity. As you take an initial walk around the location, make notes on where you feel would be the most interesting sections to concentrate your investigation.

Of course not all 'hauntings' are the result of spirit presence. There are a variety of reports where people have described ghosts appearing at the same time on the same date of a year. These are known as 'anniversary' ghosts. If you are intending visiting a location alleged to have an anniversary ghost, please go along on the relevant day, as if you do not, you may well be disappointed.

There are also lots of grey ladies, blue ladies and occasionally a green lady or two haunting Britain. Sites reporting this type of ghost are always well worth a visit as, although you may not be able to define the clothing or features of the 'lady' concerned, sightings are usually quite regular and so you are less likely to be disappointed in your quest.

Then there are the ghosts who walk through walls and disappear in the most unusual circumstances into fireplaces and the like. This happens because a spirit person visiting a former residence does not recognize any changes that have been made to the building – they perceive their former home or workplace as it was when they inhabited the mortal world. So where there was once a doorway, a door will still exist for them and they will continue to use it, thus giving the appearance of disappearing through a wall.

There are also earthbound spirits, i.e. spirits of people who have not moved on from this physical world, and the spirits of people who return in visitation to their old homes or places of work. If they wish, they may allow you to glimpse them. This may manifest itself in a number of ways. You may catch a slight movement out of the corner of your eye as you move around a place, you may see a shadow moving quickly from one part of a room to another or you may see spirit lights – bright lights flashing for a brief moment. All are signs that you are not alone.

The first thing to remember when conducting an investigation is that there are many ways in which the residents of that world beyond make their presence known to us. They may cause items to move, they may make all kinds of noises, they may brush past you or draw close to you, causing the atmosphere to chill considerably. What the investigator then has to do is confirm whether in fact there is spirit activity around or whether there is a logical and more worldly explanation for the movement of objects, the noises or the drop (or in some cases rise) in temperature. The use of a thermometer – and I would recommend the digital variety – will enable you to pinpoint temperature changes to within a degree.

Always make sure that when a noticeable temperature drop takes place you look for open windows or doors, open fireplaces or even loosely fitted window panes. All too often a draught may give rise to much excitement, only for that excitement to be dampened by the discovery that somebody has forgotten to close a door. If, after ensuring that all possible logical explanations have been dismissed, draughts are still felt moving around a room, it is more than likely that there is spirit presence there.

Parapsychologists use electromagnetic field meters to measure fluctuations in energy in an attempt to establish whether in fact there are paranormal events taking place, but I have found that EMF meters are not always capable of delivering an accurate indication of spirit presence.

The source of noises must also be examined before they can be attributed to a ghostly presence. Ensure that nobody is moving around or speaking in an adjoining room. Check to see that the noises are not emanating from the exterior of the building, i.e. cars, animals or passers-by.

Further interest can be added to an investigation by the use of audio recording equipment. Examples of electronic voice phenomenon have been widely reported in the press and you just may be fortunate enough to capture the voices of spirit entities on tape.

Another 'must have' on an investigation is camera equipment. A video recording of your experiences is a marvellous addition to your archives, but at the very least a camera of sorts should be taken along. This may enable you to capture different examples of phenomena such as orbs or traces of ectoplasm. It matters not whether the camera is of the digital or flash variety. Point it into the darkest recesses of a room at night and very often you will find that you have managed to photograph some type of paranormal phenomena.

If you are intending to hold a séance at the location it may be a good idea to place a lighted candle in the centre of the table. The flickering of the flame could indicate the movement through the atmosphere of a spirit being, but please do be careful and do not leave the candle unattended. Most importantly when holding a séance, do ask for protection from your guides and door-keepers in the world of spirit. Ask them to guard you and ensure that only the highest and the best spirit connection is made. After completing a séance, it is also important to close the circle down by sending whichever spirit people chose to call back to the light.

Apart from the above, the only other item which you have to take along to an investigation is your common sense. Do make sure that you respect the property of others. Do take along torches and spare batteries if you are visiting a location where there is no electricity connected and do wear suitable clothing and footwear.

With *Haunted Britain* guiding your footsteps around haunted locations in the United Kingdom you will have many, many hours of enjoyment to look forward to.

Good luck!

THINGS YOU SHOULD KNOW
BEFORE YOU START

What is a Ghost?

The word 'ghost' conjures up the image of a wispy wraith-like figure floating along the corridors of ancient buildings, lonely derelict monasteries or sites where historical events have taken place. In fact it is a generic word used to encompass paranormal sightings whenever they may occur. Ghosts can be ladies or gentlemen. They can be headless horsemen, tramps and crones or sprightly children. They can be dressed in modern garb. They are varied and innumerable and appear from all stages of the history of our world.

But what are ghosts? Simply, they are memories! Photographs in time! They are the result of the energy left in the fabric of a place or a building by the people who have lived, worked and died there. Today we are all imbuing the fabric of our homes and workplaces with *our* residual energies. In time to come mediums of the future will be picking up these energies and relating details of *our* lives to the people who are interested enough to listen. It will be possible for the actions of today to be picked up mediumistically by the sensitives of the future. Our daily lives leave an unseen and unwritten record in the fabric of the buildings we inhabit.

It follows of course that the more emotional the events in people's lives are, the stronger the energy they leave behind. A sensitive may pick up on the mundane day-to-day items but should something of great importance occur, whether it be great happiness or deep sadness, then the energies will be so much stronger and they will more readily tune into those energies.

This is rather well demonstrated by anniversary ghosts – those apparitions that appear at the same time on the same date in any given year. Usually they recall a tragic and untimely loss of life. Rarely do anniversary ghosts recall memories of great joy.

What is a Spirit?

A spirit is a soul. Our spirit is the part of us that lives on for ever and is eternal. Once we have shed the physical garb and passed on through what is termed 'death', we progress into the world beyond, returning to the home from whence we came. Spirit people are as alive as you and I. They are merely people who live on a faster vibration as they are not weighed down by either the physical body or the cares that plague us during our lifetime here on Earth.

It is the spirit people with whom a medium such as I connects through either clairvoyance (clear seeing) or clairaudience (clear hearing). As well as communicating directly with a medium, spirit people may also choose to communicate through that medium's spirit guide, who will then act as an intermediary, passing on messages from the people in the world beyond to their loved ones who still live in this world.

You may have heard the term 'crises ghosts'. These are not in fact ghosts but a phenomenon that occurs when at the emotionally charged moment of death the spirit projects itself into the consciousness of the person or persons who were closest to it during its lifetime here on Earth. There have been many documented occasions when people have seen a member of their family appear before them, only for them to disappear just as quickly. They have later learned of the passing to spirit of that loved one at the precise moment of their experience.

The people in the spirit world are not burdened with timetables and do not have to cope with the rigors of travel. They can be where they want when they want. They can drop into their old home to see how their family are doing or can travel to any part of the world they choose to. Just because you go on holiday or move to another part of the globe it does not mean that your family in spirit do not travel with you if they wish to. The only difference is that they don't have to find the price of a ticket!

When a medium takes part in a paranormal investigation they will, through their sensitivity to the spirit world, pick up the presence of a spirit person, but it is not beyond the realms of possibility for anyone to see a spirit if that spirit person wishes them to do so. The people from the spirit world move on a much faster vibration than we do, but by slowing down they can become visible to us all. I liken it to watching the propeller of an aeroplane. When it is static or slow moving it is clear to everyone that what is there is a very solid piece of metal. Once the engine gains momentum, the propeller vanishes from sight and all we see is a blur. We know that the propeller is there, but we just can't see it. So it is with the spirit world. Spirits only become visible to us when they choose to slow down their vibrations.

Psychic Breezes

During paranormal investigations the participants may become aware of areas of cool moving air in certain rooms. I call these 'psychic breezes' and they are caused by the movement of a spirit person around that particular room.

If a séance is held in a room where paranormal activity is recorded to have taken place, it is not unusual for the sitters to experience a feeling of coldness passing over their knees and hands as they sit generating energy in order to attract spirit presence.

In extreme cases, if an investigator is walking around an area which also contains a spirit presence, that investigator may well experience feelings of dizziness and slight nausea, or even an over-whelming flood of emotion, as they walk through the energy field of that spirit presence.

Cold Spots and Hot Spots

These two terms are commonly heard during paranormal investigations, but what do they mean? I know that parapsychologists have their own interpretation, but how they arrive at their explanations I really don't know, as they certainly don't communicate with the spirit world and indeed, in some cases, deny its very existence.

From my understanding of what I have been told by my spirit guide Sam, a cold spot is a portal or vortex, a spiritual doorway which facilitates the entry and exit of visiting spirit people into and out of our earthly atmosphere. These cold spots do not move but remain in the same area of a building. They are not to be confused with the coolness of psychic breezes, which come and go with the movement of a spirit entity.

Hot spots are the energy of a grounded spirit, i.e. a spirit person who has chosen for whatever reason to remain close to our earthly atmosphere. These spirit people remain in the surroundings that were familiar to them in their earthly life. Unlike cold spots, which remain static, hot spots move from place to place with the movement of that spirit person. The heat is caused by the energy of the grounded spirit.

ENGLAND

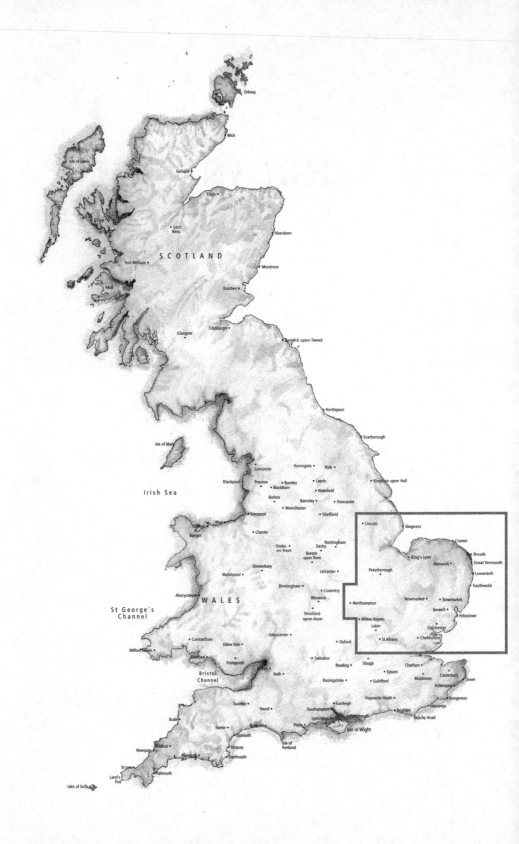

Orkney

Wick

Isle of Lewis

Golspie

Elgin

Skye

Loch Ness

Aberdeen

Fort William

SCOTLAND

Montrose

Mull

Dundee

Glasgow

Edinburgh

Berwick-upon-Tweed

Hartlepool

Scarborough

Isle of Man

Harrogate York

Lancaster

Kingston upon Hull

Blackpool Preston Leeds

Burnley Wakefield

Irish Sea Blackburn

Bolton Barnsley Doncaster

Manchester Sheffield

Liverpool

Conwy Rhyl

Chester

Lincoln Skegness

Bangor

Cromer

Nottingham

Stoke-on-Trent Derby The Broads

Burton upon Trent King's Lynn Great Yarmouth

Welshpool Shrewsbury Norwich Lowestoft

Leicester Peterborough Southwold

Aberystwyth

Birmingham Coventry

WALES Warwick Newmarket Stowmarket

Stratford-upon-Avon Northampton Ipswich Felixstowe

St George's Channel Milton Keynes Colchester

Luton

Gloucester St Albans Chelmsford

Carmarthen Ebbw Vale Oxford

Milford Haven Swindon Chatham

Swansea Reading Slough Canterbury

Pontypridd Epsom Maidstone Dover

Bristol Channel Bath Basingstoke Guildford Folkestone

Bude Taunton Yeovil Haywards Heath Dungeness

Eastleigh Hastings

Exeter Bridport Southampton Brighton Beachy Head

Newquay Bournemouth Lymington

Bodmin Exmouth Poole Isle of Wight

Torquay

St Ives Plymouth Dartmouth Isle of Portland

Land's End Falmouth

Isles of Scilly

EASTERN ENGLAND

Blisworth Tunnel, Northamptonshire

The Caxton Gibbet, Cambridgeshire

Dunwich Heath, Suffolk

Felbrigg Hall, Norfolk

Hamilton Stud Lane and Newmarket Racecourse, Suffolk

Happisburgh, Norfolk

The Lantern Man at Thurlton, Norfolk

The Battle of Naseby Battlefield, Northamptonshire

The Norfolk Broads

The Old Ferry Boat Inn, Cambridgeshire

The Old Hall Inn, Norfolk

Oliver Cromwell's House at Ely, Cambridgeshire

The St Anne's Castle, Essex

The Triangular Lodge at Rushton, Northamptonshire

The White Hart Hotel, Lincoln

Wicken Fen, Cambridgeshire

The World's End, Northamptonshire

Eastern England may not have such dramatic scenery as some parts of Britain do, but it possesses its own distinctive beauty, captured by the Suffolk painter John Constable. The region includes the famous university town of Cambridge, the historic cathedral cities of Lincoln, Norwich and Ely, North Sea coastal resorts such as Skegness and Great Yarmouth, and the picturesque waterways of the Norfolk Broads.

The eastern area known as East Anglia, which contains the reclaimed marshland of the Fens, is known for its flatness and 'big skies', and there is surely something particularly eerie about this largely featureless landscape where the horizon seems to stretch to infinity and sounds echo from miles away. This haunting atmosphere is captured perfectly by the Victorian ghost-story writer M. R. James *(see page 10)*, a Suffolk man, who used his archaeological knowledge to evoke the region's legends and myths – you may be surprised at how many supernatural secrets from the Dark Ages lurk beneath the bogs and quicksands of the Fenland.

Blisworth Tunnel

Blisworth Tunnel, on the Grand Union canal near Stoke Bruerne in Northamptonshire, is one of the longest in Britain – 3,076 yards (2.81 km) long and broad enough for two narrowboats to pass. When construction began on the Grand Junction canal, as it was then known, in 1793, the tunnel was a major feat of engineering. There were problems with alignment, but teams of navvies worked with picks and shovels for three years until they hit quicksand and the tunnel collapsed, killing 14 men.

The rest of the canal opened in 1800 and a road and tramway were built over Blisworth Hill to 'tranship' cargo from boats at either end of the collapsed tunnel. A new route was found and the tunnel finally opened on 25 March 1805, the last part of the Grand Junction canal to be completed.

The canal quickly became one of the main forms of transportation for goods from the Midlands to London, but nowadays is used mainly for pleasure cruises. However, its tragic past still lingers on. People travelling through Blisworth Tunnel have been confused by lights and a fork in the waterway, but in fact the tunnel runs straight through the hill. What people have seen is the flicker of candlelight at the spot where the first tunnel would have intersected with the main canal tunnel. The ghostly navvies are working there still…

The Boat Inn is linked to another tragedy in Blisworth Tunnel. Following a fire in the tunnel at the end of the nineteenth century, bodies were carried to the Boat and laid in the tap room.

Trips through the tunnel are available, starting from the Boat Inn, Bridge Road, Stoke Bruerne, Towcester, Northamptonshire, NN12 7SB; Tel: (01604) 862428; Website: www.boatinn.co.uk

DEREK'S TIP

If using an EMF meter in your investigation, attempt to locate any electrical wiring or equipment on the premises you have chosen, as these will adversely affect the readings of such meters.

The Caxton Gibbet

The Caxton Gibbet stands on a small knoll a mile and a half from the village of Caxton, Cambridgeshire, on what was once common land near a crossroads. Here criminals were gibbeted – imprisoned in an iron cage hanging from a gibbet until they died from starvation or exposure. Their head would be clamped at the top and their body left to putrefy for several months as a warning to others.

The gibbet at Caxton today is a replica which was probably built using the timbers of a nearby cottage. The original gibbet was blown down during a gale.

Nearby there is a Chinese restaurant, formerly an inn called the Caxton Gibbet which catered for people who came to view the gibbeting. It was also the place where the bodies were laid out after they had been cut down.

The story runs that in the eighteenth century the landlord of the inn – or possibly his son – decided to rob three wealthy travellers who were staying there. After the men had spent the night drinking and had reeled off to bed, he went into their room and started to go through their belongings. One man woke up and, in a panic, the landlord killed him. Then, to prevent the others from discovering the murder, he had to kill them too. He threw the bodies down the pub's well. Nevertheless, the travellers were missed and the landlord eventually convicted of the murder. He was hung from the gibbet within sight of his own pub.

Today the room in which the murder took place is said to be colder than the rest of the building. Footsteps have been heard walking from that room down to the foot of the stairs, which is the site of the old well.

The Caxton Gibbet is situated near the junction of the A14 and the A45, on the road from Cambridge to St Neots.

Yim Wah House Chinese Restaurant and Bar, Caxton Gibbet, Caxton, Cambridge, CB3 8PE; Tel: (01954) 718330; Website: www.yimwahhouse.com

Open seven days a week. Offers a menu from all regions of the Far East.

DEREK'S TIP

When researching a location, attempt to establish the local dialect or language of a particular spirit reputed to haunt the building. Calling out using that dialect or language may encourage a response from the spirit person or people.

Dunwich Heath

Dunwich Heath is a lowland heath on the very edge of the fast-eroding Suffolk coat. Classified as a Regionally Important Geological and Geomorphological Site (RIGS), it is one of Suffolk's most important and scenic conservation areas.

In medieval times this lonely and windswept shoreline was a busy and prosperous area. Dunwich village was a large port, similar in size to London, and the capital of East Anglia. Its thriving trade in woollen goods brought wealth, and the town had many churches, two monasteries, a bishop's palace and even a mint. All that remains today, however, is the ruins of a few cottages, a Franciscan priory and a leper hospital. Over the years, erosion of the unstable sand and flint cliffs, together with a series of violent storms, brought the village crashing down into the sea. By 1677 the sea had reached the market-place, and All Saints' Church, the final church left standing, collapsed into the sea around 1920.

With the village, according to legend, went one of the three holy crowns buried around the coastline to protect England from foreign invasion shortly after the Norman Conquest. Another of the crowns was dug up at Rendlesham, then melted down for its silver content. The third has yet to be found.

The desolate atmosphere of Dunwich Heath has inspired many ghost stories, including those of M. R. James, who grew up near Bury St Edmunds and spent holidays at Aldeburgh, just down the coast from Dunwich. He used Dunwich as the setting for one of his most famous stories, 'Oh, Whistle, and I'll Come to You, My Lad', published in 1904.

The ruins of the village themselves have a sinister reputation. Malformed figures have been seen flitting through the former leper hospital, strange lights have been seen in the old priory and it is said that the former inhabitants of the village return from the sea to walk on the clifftops. Below the waters, the sunken ruins are also believed to be haunted, and are shunned by divers. On quiet days it is said that the church bells can still be heard ringing out from beneath the sea...

Dunwich Heath, Dunwich, Suffolk, IP17 3DJ; Tel: (01728) 648501; Website: www.nationaltrust.org.uk

Dunwich Museum, St James's Street, Dunwich, Saxmundham, Suffolk, IP17 3EA; Tel: (01728) 648796. Open from the beginning of March to the end of October. The museum chronicles the history of Dunwich from Roman times.

DEREK'S TIP

Use trigger objects. These may be coins, a cross, a book or any object which lends itself easily to being placed on a plain sheet of paper and drawn around. Place the object in a sealed room, preferably with a video camera that has a lens wide enough to encompass the *whole* sheet of paper. If you are fortunate you may find that the object has been moved by a spirit entity.

Felbrigg Hall

Felbrigg Hall is one of the best-preserved seventeenth-century houses in East Anglia. Built by Robert Lyminge on the sites of a medieval property dating back to 1400, it was the home of the Windham family for over 200 years and contains many fine examples of eighteenth-century furniture and paintings. The traditional walled garden features a working eighteenth-century dovecote and the national collection of colchicums (naked ladies), which flower in September. The park is renowned for its aged trees, especially around 200 beeches. A 'Victory V' formation of 200,000 trees planted to mark VE Day can be seen from the air. There are 500 acres of woodland in total, and many way-marked woodland and lakeside walks.

The Gothic library of the hall is said to be haunted by the ghost of the second William Windham, a member of Pitt the Younger's Cabinet who inherited the estate in 1749 and began to compile the library. He was a passionate book-collector, but his love of books led to his death. In 1810, while in London, he tried to rescue a friend's books from a burning house, but fell over and injured his hip. An operation was required, but surgery was still relatively primitive at that time and it resulted in his death. However, he still returns to his old library from time to time. It is said that when his collection of Samuel Johnson's books are set out on the table, he will come back and browse through them.

Felbrigg, Norfolk, NR11 8PR; Tel: (01263) 837444; Fax: (01263) 837032; E-mail: felbrigg@nationaltrust.org.uk; Website: www.nationaltrust.org.uk

The house and gardens are open daily, apart from Thursdays and Fridays, from 19 March to 30 October.

Felbrigg village is two miles south-west of Cromer on the B1436.

Hamilton Stud Lane and Newmarket Racecourse

Hamilton Stud Lane in Newmarket is haunted by the ghost of the famous jockey Fred Archer, who rode his first flat race as a 12-year-old in 1869. He won his first classic, the 2,000 Guineas, at the age of 17, and became champion jockey the same year. He went on to become champion jockey for 13 consecutive years, from 1874 to 1886, and to win 21 classics. But success had a price. At 5 ft 10 in., he was very tall for a jockey, and only very strict dieting and a disgustingly strong purgative, known as Archer's mixture, kept him down to his racing weight of 8 st. Then misfortune struck: in 1884 his wife Nelly died in childbirth. Archer was desolate. Two years later he was 1lb overweight and lost the Cambridgeshire by a head. The effects of dieting and grief brought on a fever. Delirious, he shot himself on 8 November 1886. He was just 29 years old.

Soon after his death a local woman reported seeing Fred Archer riding down Hamilton Stud Lane towards her and her daughter and then disappearing into thin air. Since then, others have seen his ghost riding along at the same spot. It is also said that the ghost of Fred Archer haunts Newmarket Racecourse, the scene of some of his greatest triumphs. At a certain spot on the course, horses have swerved, stopped or fallen and their jockeys have reported seeing a strange white shape hanging in the air.

Newmarket Racecourse, Westfield House, The Links, Newmarket, Suffolk, CB8 0TG; Tel: (01638) 663482

Happisburgh

The village of Happisburgh (pronounced 'Hazebro') lies on the Norfolk coast. It has a beach, sand dunes and two distinctive landmarks: a tall church tower and a red and white striped lighthouse, built in 1791. It also has a unique ghost: the Pump Hill Ghost, otherwise known as the Happisburgh Torso.

One night in 1765, three smugglers at Cart Gap, Happisburgh, fell out over the division of their spoils. A fight broke out and shots were heard. The following day large pools of blood were found on the beach, but there was no body to be found.

A few months later two local farmers saw a strange figure in the vicinity of Whimpwell Street. Dressed in sailor's clothes and clutching a rough brown sack to its chest, it seemed to be walking but had no legs, and its head was dangling down its back attached only by a few thin strips of flesh. When it reached the village well it started to climb in, then suddenly disappeared.

The apparition was seen several times and the village council finally decided to investigate the well. A man was lowered into it and found a sack containing a pair of legs.

After this the well was drained and a larger sack was found. Inside was a rotting torso in sailor's clothes. Hanging from its neck, by some decomposing strips of flesh, was a skull.

Each time the well has been disturbed the Happisburgh Torso has walked. It has been seen several times moving from the shore towards the coast road with its head bouncing down its back.

Happisburgh has another ghost – he is an eighteenth-century coastguard who walks along the front, laughing.

The Lantern Man at Thurlton

Marsh gas, or the will o' the wisp, is common in the flat lands of East Anglia and has been personified as the Lantern Man. He is said to lure people to their deaths by drawing them to his light and then drowning them in thick mud and water.

At Thurlton, a village to the south of the river Yare, a gravestone to the north of All Saints' church tells of the death of wherryman Joseph Bexfield at the hands of the Lantern Man in the nineteenth century. He would take his wherry up and down the Yare between Norwich and Great Yarmouth and would often tie up for the night at Thurlton Staithe, halfway between the two, and stay at the White Horse Inn. On 11 August 1809 he was at the inn when he remembered he had left a parcel for his wife on the wherry. It was pitch dark and another of the wherrymen warned him that the Lantern Man would be out and about, but he said he knew the marsh too well to be led astray by any Jack O'Lantern. Days later his corpse was washed up between Reedham and Breydon. People say that on misty nights his ghost wanders the marshes still.

The Battle of Naseby Battlefield

The Battle of Naseby, fought in the open fields between the villages of Naseby, Sibbertoft and Clipston in Northamptonshire, was the decisive battle of the English Civil War. It started at about 9 o'clock in the morning on 14 June 1645 and lasted about 3 hours. The Royalist army numbered about 12,000 men, the Parliamentarians 15,000. The Royalists were routed and only about 4,000 escaped the field, most of whom were either cavalry or senior officers.

On the anniversary of the battle, two ghostly re-enactments take place: a convoy of grim-faced soldiers has been seen pushing carts down an old drovers' road and the entire battle has been seen taking place in the sky above the site, complete with the sounds of men screaming and cannon firing. For the first century or so after the battle villagers would come out and sit on the nearby hills to watch it.

Grid Reference: SP684799 (468490,279990); OS Landranger map: 141; OS Explorer map: 223. The battlefield is easily accessible via minor roads, though there are few rights of way.

The Norfolk Broads

The shallow waters of the Norfolk Broads are the result of medieval digging for peat. Nowadays they are a popular venue for boating and fishing. Reed-fringed Oulton Broad in Suffolk, the southern gateway to the Broads, is one of the finest yachting lakes in Britain.

Hickling Broad

Hickling is the largest of the Broads. It is a very popular spot for sailing and for fishing from boats, especially for rudd, tench and bream. The three Hickling villages – Hickling village, Hickling Green and Hickling Heath – lie to the north of the broad.

One winter during the Napoleonic Wars a poor drummer boy from Hickling home on furlough fell in love with the daughter of a rich man in Potter Heigham. Her father disapproved of the match, so the lovers met secretly in a small hut at Swim Coots in the marsh on the Heigham side of Hickling Broad. Each night the drummer boy would skate out across the frozen broad, beating on his kettle-drum to let his lover know he was coming. Then one night the drum fell silent – the boy had fallen through the ice and drowned. Since then, however, he has often been seen on February evenings, skating along and beating his drum.

Ranworth Broad

Ranworth Broad is haunted by the ghost of Brother Pacificus, who was a monk at the nearby St Benet's Abbey, a Benedictine monastery built in 816. In the 1530s he was restoring the rood-screen in Ranworth church and would row across from the abbey every day with his dog. One summer's evening when he arrived back at the abbey he found that it had been pillaged by Henry VIII's troopers and that many of the monks were dead. For many years afterwards he lived as a hermit in the abbey ruins. He is buried in Ranworth churchyard, but occasionally at dawn a monk in a black habit can still be seen rowing across the broad in a small boat with a dog sitting in the bow.

The ruins of the abbey are also haunted by a monk. At the time of the Norman Conquest, he betrayed his brethren and handed the abbey over to William the Conqueror's soldiers in exchange for the promise that he would be made abbot. He was indeed made abbot – and then nailed to the bell tower door and skinned alive by the Normans. Every 25 May he can be seen hanging there and it is said that his screaming can still be heard at other times.

Very little remains of the abbey today, but it can be visited either by river or by walking across the fields from Ludham. It lies close to the confluence of the Ant and the Bure and the remains of a windmill can be seen in the ruins of the gatehouse.

According to legend, the marshes near Ranworth Broad also see the reappearance of the Devil himself. In the eighteenth century the Old Hall, Ranworth, was the home of Colonel Thomas Sidley. He was a huntsman notorious for his hard drinking and debauchery. On New Year's Eve 1770, at the biggest meet of the season, he challenged a neighbour to a race. Unfortunately he fell behind and it was soon obvious that he was going to lose. Undeterred, he calmly shot his opponent's horse. The rider fell and broke his neck.

Later that night the colonel was celebrating his win over dinner at the Old Hall when he was interrupted by the arrival of a stranger, who threw him across his saddle and rode off into the stormy night. He was never seen again and it was claimed that it was the Devil himself who had carried him away. Every New Year's Eve it is said that he can be seen riding across the marshes with the colonel still slung across his saddle. The Old Hall has since been demolished.

The Old Ferry Boat Inn

The Old Ferry Boat Inn at Holywell, on the River Ouse, is one of the oldest in England, having originally been built in Anglo-Saxon times. The 'holy' well in the village is said to have provided Boadicea with fresh drinking water and is supposed to cure blindness.

The Old Ferry Boat is haunted by the ghost of Juliet Tewsley, who was born in the eleventh century. She fell in love with a local woodcutter, Tom Zoul, who did return her love but preferred to play ninepins with the other village lads than spend time with her. Juliet became more and more miserable as a result and one day, while Tom was drinking with his friends, she hanged herself from a willow tree beside the river. As a suicide she was not allowed to be buried in consecrated ground, so instead she was buried at a crossroads near the river with a stake through her heart and a slab of grey stone over her grave.

When the Old Ferry Boat was rebuilt, the new building was constructed on top of the grave and the stone slab became part of the flooring of the new pub. Since that time Juliet has often been seen rising from her grave and floating towards the river on 17 March, the anniversary of her death, which is known locally as Juliet's Eve. Mysterious music has been heard coming from the bar on that date, but it can only be heard by women.

The Old Ferry Boat Inn, Back Lane, Holywell, St Ives, Cambridgeshire, PE27 4TG; Tel: (01480) 463227; Website: www.oldferryboat.com

There are seven rooms, all with en-suite facilities, and a restaurant serving both traditional and more exotic food.

DEREK'S TIP

Remember that spirits do not always appear at night. They are just as likely to be in visitation during daylight hours. It is, however, far more atmospheric to conduct an investigation during the hours of darkness.

The Old Hall Inn

The seventeenth-century Old Hall Inn stands a short way away from the shore at Sea Palling, Norfolk. It was formerly a farmhouse; today it is a traditional public house with two bars, an *à la carte* restaurant, a lounge, family dining area, beer garden and several guest bedrooms.

On several occasions the figure of a woman in grey clothing has been seen sitting on a window ledge in the television lounge and a drop in temperature has been recorded.

From time to time an inexplicable bluish shadow has also appeared and there has been the smell of strong tobacco. A manager's wife once saw a 'column of grey smoke' move across the dining room towards the kitchen. This was observed on two later occasions by other witnesses.

Another of the live-in managers was often aware of a 'presence' in her flat. It seemed friendly and to delight in playing tricks – she would return to her 'empty' flat to find ornaments had been turned round and her teddy bear turned over on the bed.

In May 1975 and October 1976 a team of researchers from the Borderline Science Investigation Group investigated the inn and concluded that genuine paranormal phenomena had 'probably' occurred.

The Old Hall Inn, The Coast Road, Sea Palling, Norfolk, NR12 0TZ; Tel: (01692) 598323; Website: www.seapalling.com/oldhallinnmain.htm

Oliver Cromwell's House at Ely

Oliver Cromwell (1599–1658), Lord Protector of Great Britain, was born on 25 April 1599 at Huntingdon, the son of a country gentleman. After his marriage in London in 1620 he and his family lived first in Huntingdon and then in St Ives before moving to Ely in 1636.

The house was originally built in the thirteenth century. Between 1843 and 1869 it was an inn, the Cromwell Arms, and it is now a historic house dedicated to Cromwell.

Cromwell led the New Model Army to victory against the Royalists in the Civil War, then the Irish in 1649 and the Scots and Charles II in 1651. After dissolving the 'Rump Parliament' in 1653, he became Lord Protector. He was offered the crown in 1657, but refused it.

Although Cromwell died in London and his ghost is said to haunt Red Lion Square (see page 51), it may still return to his old home in Ely. There have been many paranormal events at the house. In 1998 a guide at the Tourist Information Centre was there when he felt a draught around his feet and realized his shoelaces were undone. In itself that wasn't particularly unusual, but every time he retied them, it happened again.

In 1979 a couple spent the night in what is now known as the haunted bedroom. During the night, the woman woke up and seemed to be in the same room but at a different time. She realized the doorway was in a different place. Then she felt her arm gripped by a large powerful man, who seemed distracted and was muttering to himself. The vision faded, but when she found herself back in her own time, the marks on her arm were still visible.

In 2003 the Cambridge Paranormal Group carried out two investigations at the house and picked up impressions of several spirits.

Oliver Cromwell`s House, 29 St Mary's Street, Ely, Cambridgeshire, CB7 4HF: Tel: (01353) 662062. Open daily all year, except Xmas Day, Boxing Day and New Year's Day.

There are videos, exhibitions and period rooms, with costumes and helmets to try on, and a gift shop. The House is also home to Ely's Tourist Information Centre.

The St Anne's Castle

Saint Anne's Castle in Great Leighs, Essex, is one of the oldest pubs in England, with parts dating to the twelfth century.

The pub is associated with the legend of a local witch, Anne Hughes, who was executed in 1621 on Scrap Faggot Green ('scrap faggot' is old Essex term for 'witch') and buried at the crossroads there with a stake through her heart and a heavy boulder on top of the grave to stop her spirit from finding its way back to the village. However, during the Second World War, American artillery trucks needed to pass through Great Leighs and moved the boulder. After that the witch apparently haunted the village and pub. One of her pranks was said to be swapping over the hens and ducks belonging to two local men during the night. A ghostly black cat which has been seen by several people over the years may belong to her.

A previous landlord of the pub had trouble with a storeroom which he could not keep tidy because items would be strewn around when no one was there. His dogs would not enter it, but the cat would. At that time drayman delivering supplies to the pub and a young girl visiting it both reported seeing a 'thing' that so upset them that they refused ever to cross the threshold again.

The current landlady has joined a ghosthunting group in an effort to learn more about the ghosts who are haunting her pub and has found out that there are a lot of them there, including a little girl with long blonde curly hair who likes cooking, a little boy who plays with her, several unfriendly monks, a woman called Elizabeth who walks around in her wedding dress, looking out of the window, and a man who sits in the bar smoking a pipe.

A ghost with a tragic story is that of George Harry Benfield, who lived in the village in the nineteenth century. He had five children, but found out that his firstborn, a son named Thomas, was his brother's child. Horrified, he killed both his wife and son by tying a piece of rope around their necks, fixing it to a piece of wood and turning the wood until their necks broke. He was later tried and hanged in Chelmsford.

As well as all these ghosts, a variety of paranormal activity has been reported in the pub, with electrical equipment turning itself on and off of its own accord and items going missing and then turning up again exactly where they had been left. One room in particular has an overpowering feeling of death and sadness. It is no exaggeration to say that the St Anne's Castle is one of the most haunted pubs in England.

The St Anne's Castle, Main Road, Great Leighs, Essex, CM3 1NE; Tel./Fax: (01245) 361253; Website: www.stannescastle.co.uk. Open all day every day.

Live music at weekends and an open mike night the first Tuesday of the month. Freshly cooked bar food and a takeaway service every lunchtime and evening.

The Triangular Lodge

The Triangular Lodge at Rushton, Northants., is a highly unusual building. Everything about it is linked to the number three. It has three 33-foot walls, each with three trefoil windows and three gables, and there are three storeys rising to a three-sided central chimney.

The lodge was designed and built by Sir Thomas Tresham between 1593 and 1597. He was a staunch Catholic and as a result was imprisoned for 15 years by the Elizabethan Protestant government. During his prolonged captivity he covered his cell walls with letters, dates, numbers and religious symbols, and on his release in 1593 he began to design the Triangular Lodge as a covert testament to his faith. All of its features – emblems, dates, gargoyles, shields and biblical passages – are said to relate to the Holy Trinity and the Catholic Mass. Thomas's son Francis was one of the Catholics later involved in the Gunpowder Plot.

Legend has it that a secret tunnel leads from the lodge and when it was discovered the owner of the lodge offered a large sum of money to anyone who would go down and investigate it. A gypsy fiddler took up the offer, but had only gone a few yards, playing his fiddle as he went, when the tunnel collapsed. Some say he died there, but others say that after a while he arrived in Australia. Either way, the sound of his ghostly fiddle has been heard coming from the ground!

The Triangular Lodge, Nr Rushton, Northants., NN14 1RG; Tel: (01536) 710761 or (01536) 205411; Website: www.english-heritage.org.uk

The lodge lies a mile west of Rushton on an unclassified road and three miles from Desborough on the A6. Parking is limited. Open Thursdays–Mondays 1 April–31 October 10 a.m.–5 p.m. No unauthorized visits at other times.

The White Hart Hotel

The White Hart Hotel is situated in the centre of medieval Lincoln, between the eleventh-century cathedral and the Norman castle. There has been an inn on this site since 1460 and the oldest part of the current building, the east wing, was built in 1710. The hotel has had many illustrious guests over the years, including the then Prince of Wales, who had lunch there in 1925, and the Yeomen of the Guard, who stayed at the hotel when the annual Maundy Thursday ceremony took place in Lincoln cathedral. More recently, the cast and crew of *The Da Vinci Code* stayed at the hotel while filming scenes in Lincoln cathedral.

There are several ghosts at the White Hart. The former stables, now the Orangery restaurant, are haunted by a highwayman who came to grief when a coachman thrust a torch into his face. Now he can be seen hiding his face in a cloak. The Orangery is noted for being unusually cold.

Another ghost is a young girl known as 'the Mobcap Girl'. She was a hotel maid who took the fancy of the hotel's ratcatcher. When she spurned his advances, he murdered her. She has since been seen cowering on the first-floor landing.

One of the hotel rooms was also the scene of an untimely death when a guest committed suicide there one Bank Holiday in the 1960s. A sad atmosphere pervades the room to this day and ghostly crying has been heard there.

Several of the hotel staff have seen an elderly lady in period costume walk down one of the corridors and disappear. In another corridor several people, including the duty manager of the hotel, have had the uneasy feeling that they were being followed, but turned to find no one there.

The White Hart Hotel, Bailgate, Lincoln, LN1 3AR; Tel: (01522) 526222; Fax: (01522) 531798; E-mail: reservations@whitehart-lincoln.co.uk; Website: www.whitehart-lincoln.co.uk

The hotel runs ghost tours for conference guests.

DEREK'S TIP

I would advise that unless you have a trained medium with you, you should not attempt to invoke spirits by using ouija boards or any similar device, especially if the location is reputed to harbour a particularly nasty spirit.

Wicken Fen

Wicken Fen is one of the last remaining undrained parts of the fens. It is Britain's oldest nature reserve and celebrated its centenary in 1999. It is a haven for wildlife – over 200 species of bird, 1,000 species of moth and butterfly, 1,000 species of beetle, nearly 2,000 species of fly, 29 species of mammal and 25 species of dragonfly have been recorded there. Charles Darwin collected beetles there in the 1820s and today 40,000 people visit the fen each year.

The fen is also visited by the ghosts of days gone by. To the north, where today Spinney Abbey Farm stands, there was once an Augustinian priory, and occasionally the sound of chanting monks can still be heard drifting across the fens. One of the monks can sometimes be seen on the path leading to the fen in the early hours of the morning. He is believed to be one of three canons who stabbed the prior, William de Lode, to death in the priory church in 1403. He wears a brown habit with the hood firmly pulled down over his face.

The flickering lights of the Lantern Man *(see page 16)* can also be seen between the farm and the bank leading to the fen.

Roman legionnaries have been reported to loom up suddenly out of the fen and phantom armies have been heard.

The most sinister ghost to haunt the fen, however, is a huge black dog with enormous eyes. According to legend, anyone who sees it will soon be dead!

Wicken Fen National Nature Reserve, Lode Lane, Wicken, Ely, Cambridgeshire, CB7 5XP; Tel./Fax: (01353) 720274; Website: www.wicken.org.uk

Wicken Fen lies south of the A1123, three miles west of Soham and nine miles south of Ely.

The visitor centre and café are open Tuesdays–Sundays and Bank Holiday Mondays. The fen is open daily, apart from Christmas Day, from dawn to dusk. Some paths are closed in very wet weather.

Formal education programmes and special events take place on a regular basis.

DEREK'S TIP

If you decide to form a circle in order to generate energy to assist spirit people in drawing close, ensure you maintain physical contact with the people who are sitting or standing on either side of you. This is important, as if contact is broken, the energy is diminished.

The World's End

The World's End pub stands in the small village of Ecton, halfway between Northampton and Wellingborough on a former toll road. The village was listed in the Domesday Book, when it was known as Echentone.

The inn was originally built in the seventeenth century and called the Globe. Royalist prisoners may have been kept in a paddock nearby after the Battle of Naseby in 1645 *(see page 17)*, which may be how it got its new name. Until recently the inn sign showed a man on a horse rearing over an abyss. The present building dates to about 1765.

Numerous stories link the artist Hogarth (1697–1764) with the World's End. It is rumoured that he once painted the inn sign but that it was stolen. It is definitely known that he visited the village and painted the portrait of a local landowner, John Palmer.

The village is also connected with the former US President Benjamin Franklin. His ancestors lived there for over 300 years and many of them were the village blacksmiths. Thomas and Eleanor Franklin, Benjamin's uncle and aunt, are buried in the churchyard.

The World's End is said to be haunted by a barmaid called Angel who worked there in the seventeenth century. She had a suitor, John, who killed her in a fit of jealous rage. Apparently he also haunts the premises, but the two spirits can't find each other!

The road outside the World's End, the A4500 between Northampton and Wellingborough, is also haunted. A nun appears there at midnight on Halloween.

The World's End, Ecton, Northants., NN6 0QN; Tel: (01604) 414521

LONDON

The Adelphi Theatre

Amen Court

The Carlton Mitre Hotel

Cleopatra's Needle

The George Inn, Southwark

Heathrow Airport

The Lyceum Theatre

The Old Vic Theatre

Osterley Park House

Red Lion Square

My good friend the historian and author Richard Jones would, I think, definitely confirm that London stands head and shoulders above all other cities in the haunted stakes. There are more ghosts per square mile in London than in any other place on Earth. This of course is due to its vastness compared to other UK cities and to its long history as the capital of England. It has long been more densely populated and that in itself produces more than the average number of ghostly happenings.

I have been a frequent visitor to London and during my career as a spirit medium investigating ghostly sightings one particular spirit person stands out in my mind. Curiously, it was not during the course of my work that I met this gentleman but whilst staying at the Carlton Mitre Hotel, which is close to Hampton Court Palace (see page 41).

The Adelphi Theatre

The Adelphi Theatre was first built in 1806 and has been rebuilt three times since. It was the first theatre to use a sinking stage and was also a pioneer of gas lighting. It seats 1,560 people and has a long tradition of staging popular musicals.

The theatre is said to be haunted by the ghost of the actor William Terris, who was stabbed outside the stage door by a minor actor named Richard Arbor Prince on 16 December 1897. Prince is said to have been jealous of Terris's success and to have bought the dagger some time earlier in order to kill him as soon as he had the chance.

As Terris lay dying in the street his mistress rushed out and held him in her arms. He whispered to her, 'I'll be back.' Since then he has been seen several times in the theatre, in the nearby Covent Garden tube station, which was built on the site of his favourite baker's shop, in Maiden Lane and possibly in the Lyceum Theatre as well *(see page 46)*. He wears a grey suit and white gloves and has been seen walking through a whole row of seats and disappearing through a wall. One evening several men were working in the theatre when they saw a glowing green light which turned into the misty figure of the former actor. He floated across the stage and into the stalls. Rapping noises have also been heard in the dressing room Terris used. Apparently he used to tap on the door of an adjoining room to let his leading lady know that he was going out for a few minutes.

Richard Arbor Prince was certified insane and confined to a mental institution.

The Adelphi Theatre, The Strand, London WC2E 7NA; Tel: 020 7344 0055

DEREK'S TIP

If possible, take along with you more than one video camera, as this will increase your chances of capturing ghostly activity on film.

Amen Court

Amen Court is a small alleyway close to St Paul's cathedral. It backs onto the site of the former Newgate prison. It is thought that many prisoners tried to escape from Newgate by climbing over the wall into the court. It was also the site of the prison's scaffold, where 12 men could be executed at the same time, and the lime pits where their remains were buried.

Now the alley is known as 'Dead Man's Walk' because so many people have seen a dark shapeless figure sliding along the wall and heard the sound of clanking chains. It is thought that this may be the ghost of Jack Sheppard, an infamous cat burglar who escaped from Newgate three times before finally being hanged in November 1724.

The ivy-covered wall at the end of Amen Court is haunted by 'the Black Dog of Newgate'. Just before a prisoner was hanged this ghostly dog was said to glide up and down the alley, accompanied by a sickening smell, and crawl along the top of the wall. It is said that it first appeared in the thirteenth century, when a famine hit London and a scholar charged with sorcery was killed and eaten by his fellow prisoners. However, he had his revenge one night soon afterwards, when the mysterious dog appeared, dripping blood from its jaws, and tore them limb from limb. Though the prison was demolished in 1902, people still claim to have seen the dog crawling across the wall, dropping into the courtyard and disappearing into thin air.

Amen Court, London EC4

The Carlton Mitre Hotel

The Carlton Mitre Hotel stands on the banks of the River Thames, directly opposite Hampton Court Palace. Parts of the hotel date back to 1665 and it was originally a lodging-house for courtiers who could not be accommodated at Hampton Court Palace. It was renovated in 1993.

The hotel has a restaurant, Hamptons, with excellent river views, also a riverside bar/brasserie, which has a secluded terrace and private moorings. It can also offer excellent facilities for business travellers, with a business centre and a range of rooms available for meetings, seminars and conferences.

During a stay here I regularly 'bumped into' a gent dressed in Elizabethan attire who Sam informed me was called Edward. This small snippet of information was all that I received, but I was taken by the frequency of Edward's appearances and by the manner in which he conducted himself – he noticed none of the changes that must have taken place over the long years since he had walked the Earth plane, just carried on as he had over 400 years ago. He was happy.

I suppose that Edward still wanders around the hotel, still oblivious to the fact that we are now in the twenty-first century.

The Carlton Mitre Hotel, Hampton Court Road, Hampton Court, London KT8 9BN; Tel: 020 8979 9988

Cleopatra's Needle

Cleopatra's Needle is a 60 ft tall Egyptian obelisk which stands on the Thames Embankment between Waterloo Bridge and Hungerford Bridge. It was made for Pharaoh Thotmes III in 1475 BC and given to the British by the Turkish Viceroy of Egypt in 1819. It is known as Cleopatra's Needle as it came from Alexandria, Cleopatra's royal city. It was brought to London in 1878 to commemorate the British victory over Napoleon 63 years earlier.

Some say Cleopatra herself cursed the Needle, and its journey to Britain was certainly fraught with danger. An initial attempt to move the Needle failed when it toppled over into the sand. It remained there for many years until a cigar-shaped container ship, called the *Cleopatra*, was specially designed, at great expense, to carry it to London. The *Cleopatra* was towed by a steamship, the *Olga*, but in a storm off the Bay of Biscay she nearly sank. The *Olga* sent six volunteers to rescue the crew, but their boat sank and they all drowned. They are commemorated today on one of the plaques at the base of the Needle. The *Cleopatra*'s crew was eventually taken off by the *Olga*, and the *Cleopatra* herself, with the Needle, was cut adrift on the stormy sea. Five days later she was spotted floating off the north coast of Spain and was towed into the port of Ferrol. Another steamship, the *Anglia*, finally towed her home.

Today four plaques at the base of the Needle give a brief history of the Needle and it is flanked by two large bronze Victorian sphinxes. Underneath it lies a Victorian time capsule containing a set of coins, a newspaper, a razor, a box of pins, four Bibles, a railway guide and 12 photos of Victorian beauties. During World War I the plinth and one of the sphinxes sustained damage during a Zeppelin air raid. This can still be seen today. The Needle has a twin, which now stands in Central Park, New York.

It is not the Needle itself that is haunted, but the area surrounding it. Mocking laughter and anguished cries have been heard there and most of the suicides that take place along this stretch of the river occur at this particular spot, which some say is due to the encouragement of the spirit voices.

The ghost of one of the suicides has been seen on many occasions. He is a tall naked man who runs from behind the Needle, jumps onto its base and throws himself into the river without making a splash.

Cleopatra's Needle, Victoria Embankment, London SW1

The George Inn

The George Inn in Southwark is the only galleried coaching inn left in London. There were once many such inns, but with the coming of the railways most were demolished. The George itself had a narrow escape. The Great Northern Railway used it as a depot and pulled down two of its fronts to build warehousing before a public outcry resulted in the preservation of the south face. Now the George serves as a pub and restaurant and even a stage set for Shakespeare's plays. The ground floor is divided into a series of connecting bars. The Old Bar was the former waiting room and the Middle Bar was the coffee room. This was a haunt of Charles Dickens and the George is mentioned in his novel *Little Dorrit*.

The George's ghost is believed to be a former landlady, Miss Murray. She kept the pub for 50 years in the late nineteenth and early twentieth centuries and has since been seen floating around its rooms. She seems to be averse to modern technology, for computers crash in the pub, new tills malfunction and digital cameras often fail to take any pictures at all.

The George Inn, 77 Borough High Street, Southwark, London SE1 1NH; Tel: 020 7407 2056

Heathrow Airport

Heathrow Airport lies 15 miles west of London. It is Britain's largest airport and also the scene of several hauntings. Airline employees have often reported feeling hot breath upon their necks and hearing a man howling and barking like a dog. When they have turned round, no one has been there. This ghost is believed to be that of the highwayman Dick Turpin, who was hanged in 1739 and apparently enjoyed playing jokes like this when he was alive.

Inevitably there are also the ghosts of people who have died in plane crashes. One foggy night in March 1948 a Belgian Airlines DC3 Dakota crashed on approach into Heathrow. All 22 people on board were killed, but as the rescue crews were sorting through the wreckage a man in a hat emerged from the fog and asked if they had found his briefcase. As they stared at him, he faded away. They later found his body in the wreckage. Since that night he has been seen many times. He apparently appears out of nowhere and walks along the runway as if still searching for his briefcase.

Another businessman who haunts the airport also seems worried. He wears a grey suit and haunts one of the VIP lounges. Sometimes he simply appears from the waist down.

London Heathrow Airport, 234 Bath Road, Harlington, Middlesex, UB3 5AP; Tel: 0870 000 0123; Fax: 020 8745 4290; Website: www.heathrowairport.com

The Lyceum Theatre

The Lyceum is a Grade II listed theatre in the heart of London with a capacity of over 2,000. The original theatre built on the site opened in 1772, but was razed to the ground by fire in 1830. It reopened in 1834, having been rebuilt with the now familiar porticoed frontage. It was renamed The Royal Lyceum and English Opera House, though generally it remained known simply as The Lyceum.

The theatre gained the reputation of being unlucky after a number of owners went bankrupt, but its fortunes changed after American 'Colonel' Bateman took over, assembling a new company headed by the great actor Henry Irving. Irving's performance as Hamlet in 1874 ran over 200 nights, an unheard of success in its day.

Most of that theatre was eventually demolished due to lack of funding to implement new fire regulations, though the portico and façade were retained as part of the current theatre, which opened in 1904. Once again there was a notable performance of *Hamlet* on the premises, this time by Sir John Gielgud in 1939. In the same year plans for a road extension and roundabout threatened the future of the theatre, but they were eventually scrapped and after the Second

World War the theatre became a dance hall and then a music venue. It now hosts large-scale musicals.

The ghostly figure of a woman has often been seen in the stalls area holding a man's severed head. This is supposed to be the head of Henry Courtenay, the local landowner who was beheaded on the orders of Oliver Cromwell at the time of the Civil War.

The actor William Terris is also supposed to have been seen in the theatre *(see page 38)*.

The Lyceum Theatre, 21 Wellington Street, London WC2E 7RQ; Tel: 0870 243 9000 (box office)

DEREK'S TIP

An obvious item for investigating at night is a torch but remember to take a supply of batteries too – mischievous spirits like nothing more than to drain battery power, leaving you literally in the dark!

The Old Vic Theatre

The Old Vic was built in 1818 and was known as the Royal Coburg Theatre until 1833. On its opening night it presented a melodrama, an Asiatic ballet and a harlequinade, and today it continues to present a wide range of work from classic drama to innovative contemporary work.

Despite being described as a 'a licensed pit of darkness, a trap of temptation, profligacy and ruin' by Charles Kingsley in the 1850s, the theatre has considerably influenced dramatic art. It is said to be haunted by the ghost of Lillian Baylis, who managed the theatre in the early twentieth century, and Eric Ross, an actor who died during the Spanish 'flu epidemic of 1917–18. There have also been reports of a distraught actress re-enacting the sleepwalking scene from *Macbeth*.

The Old Vic Theatre, The Cut, Waterloo Road, London SE1 8NB; Tel: 0870 060 6628 (box office), 020 7928 2651 (administration); Fax: 020 7261 9161; Website: www.oldvictheatre.com

Osterley Park House

Osterley Park House, set in 357 acres of garden, parkland and farmland just off the A4 in Hounslow, west London, was originally built by Sir Thomas Gresham, Queen Elizabeth I's financial adviser, in 1562. In 1683 it was bought by Nicholas Barbon, who used it as security to raise a large sum of money, but the house fell into disrepair and Barbon himself died in debt. In 1713 the house was acquired by Sir Francis Child, the founder of Child and Co. bank, in payment of the loan, and it became the Child family's country house. In 1761 Sir Francis's grandson, also called Francis, commissioned leading architect Robert Adam to transform it into the elegant neo-classical villa that can be seen today.

The ghost at Osterley is known as 'the lady in white'. She is a beautiful lady in a white flowing dress who appears near the left-hand arch under the main stairway leading to the entrance of the house. She then moves towards the doorway and disappears. She usually makes her appearance at 4.30 in the afternoon and has been seen by both estate workers and visitors to the house.

The lady's identity is not known for certain, but it is possible that she is the ghost of Sarah Anne Child, the family's sole heir, who eloped to Gretna Green in 1782, when she was 18, with John Fane, son of the ninth Earl of Westmorland. Her father was so angry at the marriage that he changed his will so that the estate did not pass to the Westmorland family. Eventually it was inherited by Sarah's daughter Sarah Sophia Fane and passed down her family until it was given to the National Trust in 1949.

Today the house and grounds are open to the public. There is a tea room, shop, farm shop and educational facilities, and the property may be hired for weddings and private functions.

Osterley Park House, Jersey Road, Isleworth, Middlesex, TW7 4RB; Tel: 020 8232 5050 (visitor services), (01494) 755566 (info line); Fax: 020 8232 5080; Website: www.nationaltrust.org.uk

Red Lion Square

Red Lion Square, in the West End, is said to be haunted by three famous parliamentarians: Oliver Cromwell, John Bradshaw and Henry Ireton. They were all involved in sentencing King Charles I to death at the end of the Civil War. Bradshaw was president of the trial and was afterwards appointed Permanent President of the Council of State and Chancellor of the Duchy of Lancaster by Cromwell. Cromwell himself became Lord Protector and his son-in-law Henry Ireton was appointed Lord Deputy.

After the Restoration of the monarchy in 1660, a court was appointed to try those regicides who were still alive. Ten were found guilty and were sentenced to be hung, drawn and quartered. Ireton had died in 1651, Cromwell in 1658 and Bradshaw in 1659, but they were all posthumously tried for high treason, found guilty and also sentenced to be hung, drawn and quartered. In January 1661 their corpses were exhumed from Westminster Abbey, dragged to the gallows at Tyburn, hung in chains and decapitated. The decomposing heads were then displayed on poles outside Westminster Hall, while the rest of their remains were thrown into a pit in a field. This has since become Red Lion Square and the ghostly parliamentarians have been seen walking across it, deep in conversation.

See also Oliver Cromwell's House at Ely, page 23.

Red Lion Square, London WC1R

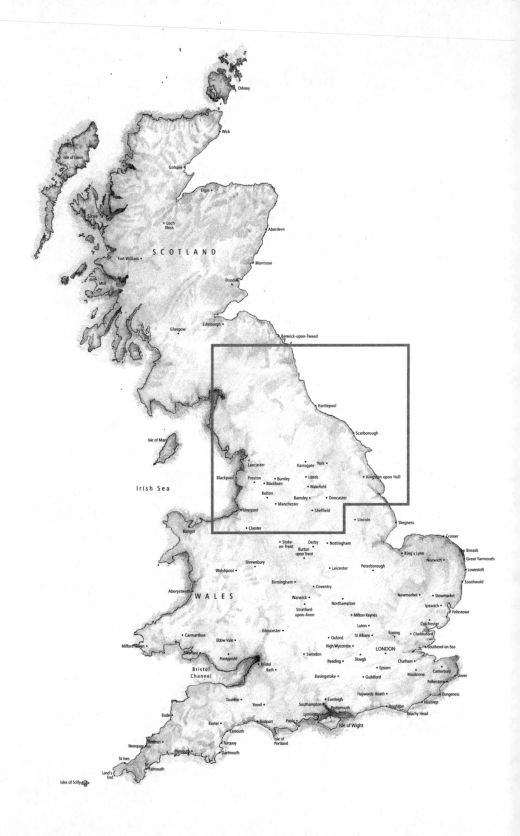

NORTHERN ENGLAND

Barrock Fell, Cumbria

The Black Swan, York

The Civic Theatre, Darlington

Clifford's Tower, York

The Coach and Horses Hotel, Chester

Dunstanburgh Castle, Northumberland

East Riddlesden Hall, Yorkshire

Kirkstone Pass Inn, Cumbria

Marston Moor Battlefield, Yorkshire

The National Railway Museum, York

The Octagon Theatre, Bolton

The Old Original, Oldham

Pontefract Castle, Yorkshire

The Prospect Shopping Centre, Hull

The Shakespeare Public House, Manchester

The Snickleway Inn, York

Tynemouth Priory and Castle, Tyne and Wear

Tyneside Cinema, Newcastle upon Tyne

Whitby Abbey, Yorkshire

Winter's Gibbet, Northumberland

Ye Olde Black Boy, Hull

Ye Olde Man and Scythe Inn, Bolton

I am a northern lad, so how could I not love northern England? I was born in Liverpool in the north-west and that city itself abounds with stories of hauntings and ghostly sightings. I have conducted one or two investigations in Liverpool around the Rodney Street area (as documented in *The Psychic Adventures of Derek Acorah*) and I can guarantee that anybody who is looking to visit this city on a ghost-hunting expedition will not be disappointed.

Of course there are many other towns and cities in the north of England where a plethora of ghosts walk. Travel north following the M6 to the ancient town of Lancaster with its castle and history of the Lancashire Witches, then go to the Lake District and beyond to Carlisle. Turn right and follow Hadrian's Wall through Northumberland. How can anybody who is looking for a paranormal experience be short of locations to investigate? But of course my heart will always belong to Liverpool and its haunted history.

Barrock Fell

Barrock Fell, in Cummersdale, to the south of Carlisle, was occupied by the Romans in the late fourth century. They built a small fort and signal station there, possibly to guard the important road to the south.

The fell is not haunted by Romans, however, but by a notorious highwayman, John Whitfield of Cotehill, who terrorized the neighbourhood in the mid-eighteenth century. Finally, in 1768, a young boy witnessed him shooting a man called William Cockburn on the road near Armithwaite and he was caught, tried and sentenced to be gibbeted on Barrock Fell. Hanging in his iron cage and starving to death, he cried out in agony for several days until a mail coachman passing by finally put him out of his misery by shooting him. Now it is said that his ghost can still be heard crying out in torment.

Barrock Fell, Cummersdale, Carlisle, Cumbria

The Black Swan

The Black Swan is one of York's most traditional pubs. It has a medieval timber-framed exterior and a classical seventeenth-century interior. It was originally built in 1417 and for many years was the home of the Bowes family. William Bowes was Lord Mayor of York in 1417 and 1428, and Sir Martin Bowes became jeweller to Queen Elizabeth I and the Lord Mayor of London. There may have been a secret side to this eminent family, for there is evidence of a secret passage leading from the house to St Cuthbert's church and of a secret room, which may have been used for cock fighting. The first record of the house being used as a pub was in 1763.

Today the Black Swan offers pub lunches, live folk music and two *en-suite* bedrooms, each with a separate annex for children. A function room is available for business meetings and special occasions.

Several ghosts have been reported in the Black Swan. A beautiful young woman in a long white dress has been seen staring into the fire, her face hidden by long black hair, and a Chaplinesque figure in a bowler hat wanders aimlessly through the rooms as though waiting for someone. The strangest ghost is a pair of male legs!

The Black Swan, Peasholme Green, York, North Yorkshire, YO1 7PR; Tel: (01904) 686911

The Civic Theatre

The Civic Theatre, Darlington, formerly the New Hippodrome and Palace of Varieties, opened in 1907. Its first managing director was Signor Rino Pepi, an Italian who was originally a quick-change artist and impersonator. He had a small bed-sitting room and kitchen, now the telephone sales office, behind the door to the left of his box. He would often enter his box through this door, accompanied by his wife and beloved Pekinese dog. He died in November 1927, but is supposed to haunt the theatre to this day, along with his dog. Staff claim he has tapped them on the shoulder in order to make his presence known.

The theatre is also haunted by the ghost of a flyman who hanged himself there. A flyman is a technician who raises or lowers – or 'flies' – the scenery by means of ropes. Many of the techniques used are similar to those used on sailing ships and it was once common for former sailors to work as flymen. There have also been sightings of the ghost of a young ballerina in the theatre.

A team of psychic investigators from Yorkshire recently spent a night carrying out tests on the premises and apparently detected several ghosts, including those of Signor Pepi, an unhappy young girl and a dog. The body of a dog was later found buried near the building.

The Civic Theatre, Parkgate, Darlington, County Durham, DL1 1RR; Tel: (01325) 486555 (enquiries), (01325) 486555 (box office). Guided tours of the theatre are available on request and ghost tours are run from time to time.

Clifford's Tower

York is reputed to be one of the most haunted towns in Britain and Clifford's Tower, one of its most famous landmarks, is notorious for the strange phenomena that have taken place there.

The tower was originally built in wood by William the Conqueror during his campaign to subdue the north of England. In 1190 it was the scene of one of the most terrible events in York's history. Anti-Semitism swept through the town and many of the large Jewish community fled their homes and sought refuge in the tower. However, the mob caught up with them there and offered them the choice of being baptized or murdered. Most chose to commit suicide and the remainder were massacred when the rioters stormed the tower and set it on fire.

In the thirteenth century the tower was rebuilt by Henry III, using stone from a nearby quarry. Not long afterwards people reported a red fluid oozing from the walls. It was thought to be the blood of those who had died there, though scientific tests have since revealed that it was probably the result of iron oxide in the stone. Yet strangely none of the other stone taken from the quarry contained iron oxide.

Staff in the tower today often feel they are being watched, even when they are on their own, and in the chapel several people have felt the touch of a ghostly hand on their shoulder. A team of psychic investigators recently held a ghost watch at the tower and claimed to have found the spirits of a young boy, a man and two dogs there.

Clifford's Tower, Tower Street, York, North Yorkshire, YO1 9SA; Tel: (01904) 621756 (event line), (01904) 621756 (info line)

DEREK'S TIP

I find it so much better if you keep the same group of people in your investigative team. By doing this you are building up trust in one another and can rely on everybody not to embellish or enhance any sightings or findings.

The Coach and Horses Hotel

The Coach and Horses Hotel is a traditional pub and hotel in the heart of the historic Roman city of Chester. It has a very strange tale of haunting.

One hot summer's evening in 1988 an old gentleman in a tweed suit came into the pub and sat down near the side entrance. He ordered a drink and sat quietly for a while on his own. When the barmaid asked if he was alright, he said he was, then came over to the bar, ordered another drink and started to talk to her. He explained that his wife had died suddenly and he wasn't looking forward to going home, because everything there reminded him of her. He asked if there was a room free at the hotel. There was, so the elderly gentleman paid cash and the barmaid booked him in and gave him his key. He drained his drink and said he would take a walk around the city walls before coming back. With a smile, he left the inn.

When he hadn't returned by 2 o'clock in the morning, the hotel staff began to worry that something had happened to him and rang the police. After searching the city in vain, the police went to the address that the man had given in Birkenhead. Neighbours told them that he had lived there and his wife had died suddenly, but so had he – eight years ago!

The Coach and Horses Hotel, 39 Northgate Street, Chester, CH1 2HQ; Tel: (01244) 325533

Dunstanburgh Castle

The windswept skeleton of Dunstanburgh Castle, the largest castle in Northumberland, lies nine miles north-east of Alnwick, dominating the coastline from its position high on an outcrop of the Great Whin Sill. It was built in the fourteenth century during the border wars between Scotland and England by Thomas, Earl of Lancaster, nephew of King Edward II. Unfortunately relations between the two broke down and Thomas eventually led a barons' rebellion against the king. He was captured and executed at Pontefract Castle *(see page 70)* in 1322, but the executioner was inexperienced and took 11 strokes to sever his head. Even soldiers fainted at the sight. Now his ghost is said to walk the ruins of Dunstanburgh Castle carrying his mangled head.

By the sixteenth century the castle had fallen into decay, but according to legend when a knight called Sir Guy sought shelter there in a storm, the drawbridge was lowered and a hideous figure in white appeared and asked him to enter and find a 'beauty bright'. Sir Guy entered an ornate chamber where he found 100 knights and their horses lying asleep. In the middle of the room a beautiful woman lay sleeping in a crystal casket. On either side of her were two serpents, one holding a sword, the other a horn. The ghostly figure told Sir Guy he could wake the woman but must choose whether to use the sword or the horn to do so. He chose the horn, but as he blew it, the knights woke instead and rushed towards him. Sir Guy fainted clean away and when he came round the vision had gone. For the rest of his life he searched the ruins for the beautiful maiden, but he never found her again. Now his ghost continues the search.

Dunstanburgh Castle, Craster, Alnwick, Northumberland; Tel: (01665) 576231; www.english-heritage.org.uk

Open daily April–October and Thursday–Monday November–March. Closed 24–26 December and 1 January.

The castle can be reached by foot from Embleton and Craster. Car parking is available at both. There is a small shop.

East Riddlesden Hall

East Riddlesden Hall is a seventeenth-century merchant's house a mile north-east of Keighley. It stands in its own grounds, which include gardens, a duck pond, an orchard and one of the largest medieval tithe barns in the north of England.

The hall is haunted by four ghosts. Perhaps the best known is a Grey Lady who was starved to death by her husband and who now rocks an ancient cradle. The other ghosts are those of a Scottish merchant murdered by a steward for his money, a White Lady who haunts the pond where she drowned and a Blue Lady who haunts the grounds.

East Riddlesden Hall, Riddlesden, Bradford Road, Keighley, North Yorkshire, BD20 4EA; Tel: (01535) 607075; Fax: 01535 691462; E-mail: eastriddlesden@ntrust.org.uk; Website: www.visitbrontecountry.com/erh.htm

Open April–November. The hall is run by the National Trust. It has free parking, a shop, tea room, children's play area and educational facilities. Regular costumed tours and a variety of events are held through the year.

Kirkstone Pass Inn

Kirkstone Pass Inn is a well-known inn dramatically situated on the Kirkstone Pass between Ullswater and Windermere. At 1,500 feet, it is believed to be the third highest public house in England and it is a favourite with walkers and other visitors to the Lake District.

The inn is said to be haunted by a seventeenth-century coachman. He hangs around the bar as if reluctant to go back out into the hills and continue his journey. Travel was often hazardous in past times, as shown by the fate of the other ghost at the inn, a young woman who died of exposure while travelling over the pass during a blizzard.

Kirkstone Pass Inn, Kirkstone Pass, Ambleside, Cumbria, LA22 9LQ; Tel: (01539) 433888. Food served. Accommodation available.

Marston Moor Battlefield

Marston Moor lies beyond the southern end of Nidderdale in the Vale of York, about a mile north of Long Marston and to the east of Tockwith. It was the site of a major battle in the Civil War.

On the evening of 2 July 1644 a Royalist army of 15,000 soldiers under the command of William Cavendish, later Duke of Newcastle, and Prince Rupert of the Rhine, King Charles I's nephew, met an army of 25,000 allied Parliamentarian and Scots troops under the overall command of Alexander Leslie, Earl of Leven, and Generals Thomas Fairfax and Oliver Cromwell. The Royalist commanders had been convinced that battle would not take place until the following morning and been surprised by the Allied attack. The battle lasted for two hours, lit by moonlight. After initial success, the Royalists were defeated and their northern army destroyed.

As night fell, 300 Allied soldiers and 4,000 Royalists lay dead. The Allied dead were respectfully buried by their comrades, but the Royalists were robbed and stripped and the Parliamentarians forced the villagers of Tockwith and Long Marston to dump the bodies in a pit. Marston Moor is now peaceful farmland, but the ghostly battle continues to this day. Royalist cavalry has been seen charging across the fields and there have been many sightings of phantom soldiers walking along the road between Long Marston and Tockwith which runs across the centre of the battlefield. A monument commemorating the battle has been erected halfway along this road, next to a layby.

Marston Moor lies off the B1224 to the west of Tockwith, Vale of York.

The National Railway Museum

The National Railway Museum is the largest railway museum in the world. It traces the history of the railway industry from the early nineteenth century, when George and Robert Stephenson developed *Rocket*. Alongside a large collection of photographs there are millions of railway artefacts and many railway vehicles, including the famous *Flying Scotsman*, *Mallard*, which holds the world speed record for a steam train, the only bullet train outside Japan and a host of royal carriages, including Queen Victoria's.

There are often special *Thomas the Tank Engine* days for children, and rides on the miniature railway or full-size trains are usually available.

There are also rumours of ghostly activity in the travelling post office, where mail used to be sorted and then dropped off at stations in sacks as the train raced through the country.

The National Railway Museum, Leeman Road, York, North Yorkshire, YO26 4XJ; Tel: (01904) 621261; Fax: (01904) 611112; Website: www.nrm.org.uk

Open all year, every day except 24, 25 and 26 December. Admission free except for some activities during special events.

The Octagon Theatre

The Octagon Theatre, Bolton, was established in 1967. It presents two seasons of shows per year with a wide range of both home-produced and touring productions, including musicals, classics and comedies. Although the theatre is actually hexagonal, the main auditorium is an elongated octagon. It seats up to 380 people. The building also houses the Bill Naughton Theatre (an 80-seat adaptable studio theatre), the Spotlight Café and a theatre bar.

The theatre's ghost is its first wardrobe mistress, Fida, who died while she was working there. She has been seen strolling across the gallery and in the stage control box and has even appeared to operate the sewing machines from time to time!

The Octagon Theatre, Howell Croft South, Bolton, BL1 1SB; Tel: (01204) 520661; Website: www.octagonbolton.co.uk

The Old Original

The Old Original is a traditional pub in the former mill town of Oldham. It is haunted by a woman called Eliza Jane MacKay, who lived in the area in the nineteenth century and was a regular drinker at the inn. She came to a bad end one night when she was murdered and thrown down the local well, 800 yards down the lane from the pub. Each year on a certain night in May people in the houses nearby can hear the sound of screaming. This may be a re-enactment of Eliza being dragged screaming from the pub to the well. The inquest took place in July and the *Oldham Chronicle*'s account of it is on the wall in the pub today. Eliza herself is also still around her old haunt, appearing as an ill-defined shadowy shape and always passing through the same part of the inn. It seems she haunts the cellar too, as things are often turned on and off down there.

The Old Original, Thurston Clough Road, Scouthead, Oldham, Lancashire, OL4 3RX; Tel: (01457) 874412. Food served.

Pontefract Castle

Pontefract Castle, built in 1090, was one of the most important fortresses in England during the Middle Ages. It became a royal castle in 1399, upon the accession of Henry Bolinbroke to the throne. He imprisoned his predecessor, Richard II, in the castle and had him murdered the following year. During the Civil War the castle was held by Royalists forces through three sieges, but was largely demolished by the victorious Parliamentarians at the end of the war.

No one has yet seen the ghost of Richard II at the castle – though a photograph of the keep once showed a ghostly figure wearing a crown – but it is known to be the haunt of many other ghosts. Visitors have often seen a black monk walking from the kitchen towards the steps up to the Queen's Tower at around 5 o'clock in the afternoon. A grey monk has also been seen and a woman wearing grey walks regularly from Stoney Hill to the castle gates, sometimes holding a lantern.

Another ghost has been seen reflected in a mirror at the visitors' centre. She is a young girl with long brown hair, dressed in ragged clothes. Unexplained sounds of a girl crying and screaming have been reported in the ladies' toilet which adjoins the visitors' centre.

Strange knocking has also been heard in the castle's underground magazine, which held gunpowder and prisoners during the Civil War. A shadowy figure has been seen descending the stairs to the magazine and cavaliers have been seen coming up them and walking off to various parts of the castle. Two phantom children have been seen playing near the entrance, while on top of the keep a man dressed in black has been observed reading a parchment. Though the castle is now in ruins, it seems there is still a lot going on there.

Pontefract Castle, Castel Chain, Pontefract, West Yorkshire, WF8 1QH; Tel: (01977) 723440. Open daily.

DEREK'S TIP

If your investigation is to take place at night, ensure that you have warm clothing and the facility to make hot drinks. Remember that even the warmest of summer days can turn chilly after the witching hour.

The Prospect Shopping Centre

The Prospect Shopping Centre, Hull, has a wide selection of high street and department stores and places to eat. The site was once the venue for public executions. Subsequently the Hull Royal Infirmary was built there. It opened on 1 September 1784 and remained on the same site for 183 years until the new Hull Royal Infirmary opened in Anlaby Road. The old building was then demolished and the land allocated to the development of a new shopping centre.

The new complex opened in the mid-1970s and ever since there have been reports of strange events taking place on the premises. Canteen utensils and waste bins have been strewn around, stock has been moved inexplicably and several items have appeared in unusual places and been uncannily cold to the touch. When one shop opened the staff posed for a photo and when it was developed they saw that an extra person no one recognized had been standing there with them.

It is believed that the ghosts haunting the shopping centre are those of hospital patients and workers. Staff working late in the offices have seen the shadowy figures of hospital porters dressed in 'whites'. One porter is said to have been around since the 1930s, when he committed suicide in the porters' lodge. A nurse in an old-fashioned uniform was also seen by a woman working late in one of the shops, but when she approached her, she walked behind a column and disappeared.

The Prospect Shopping Centre, Brook Street, Hull, HU2 8PP; Tel: (01482) 324619; Fax: (01482) 325640

The Shakespeare Public House

The Shakespeare is now located in the centre of Manchester, but in the 1920s the entire pub was transported from Chester, where it was known as the Shambles. It dates back to 1656 and still has the original black and white façade, old wooden floors and oak beams.

It also still has its ghost. She is said be a kitchen maid who lived in the nineteenth century and died after being raped by the chef, who later hanged himself. The rope marks are still there on an old beam.

The Shakespeare, 16 Fountain Street, Manchester, M2 2AA; Tel: 0161 834 5515

Food is available in the pub or upstairs in the restaurant, which can also be booked for private parties.

The Snickleway Inn

A snickleway is an alleyway, and the Snickleway Inn in York is a traditional pub in a building which dates back to medieval times, when the old town was full of narrow passageways. It was renovated around 1580 and the timber framing of the Tudor and Jacobean rooms can still be seen. Rumour has it that it was once a brothel, but it has been linked with the pub trade since the seventeenth century.

As may be expected with an old building with a colourful past, there are several ghosts haunting the premises. An old man has been seen entering the pub through the old back door – which is now blocked up – and sitting down before disappearing into thin air. He ran the pub at the turn of the nineteenth century. The current licensees have seen him twice. He is not always visible, but can often be heard grunting. Another former licensee and her cat also apparently haunt the bar and an Elizabethan man in a blue doublet has also been seen there.

The stairs are said to be haunted by the ghost of a four-year-old girl who was killed by a brewer's dray and by a young nun who broke her vows and had a child. A baby has been heard crying in the pub when there are no children present.

A feeling of evil has been reported in the cellar and a medium who once investigated the premises sensed a presence there.

Sometimes the whole pub is pervaded by the smell of lavender. During the Great Plague, which killed 3,512 people in York in 1604, lavender was used to mask the smell of rotting corpses.

The ghost of Marmaduke Buckle is said to roam between a first-floor room in the Snickleway and the house next door, which is now a restaurant and tea room. Marmaduke lived a sad life in the seventeenth century – he was physically handicapped and was accused of witchcraft, so he spent most of his life shut away. By the time he was 17, he had had enough. He carved his initials, birth and death dates on a beam and hanged himself.

The Snickleway Inn, 47 Goodramgate, York, North Yorkshire, YO1 7LS; Tel: (01904) 656138.

The Snickleway has possibly the smallest beer garden in England. Food is served at lunchtime.

DEREK'S TIP

A more sceptical member of the group is useful in providing 'the voice of reason'. It is very easy to attribute every squeak or groan to spirit activity when in fact the source could well be something as mundane as the building cooling down at night or the floorboards relaxing after constant use during the day.

Tynemouth Priory and Castle

Tynemouth's castle and priory church stand on a headland looking out over the North Sea and guarding the approach to the River Tyne. The priory was founded in 617 and was the burial place of the early Northumbrian kings. It was destroyed by the Danish invasions of the ninth century and the present building dates to 1090. The castle was added in the fourteenth century for defensive purposes. Over the centuries both priory and castle have been used as landmarks and served as important fortifications against the Vikings, Scots and the armies of Napoleon. There is a monument here to Admiral Collingwood, a local Battle of Trafalgar hero. During both world wars the castle was used as a coastal defence and the restored magazines of the gun battery can still be seen.

Nowadays much of the priory church remains, though most of the domestic outbuildings of the monastery have disappeared. Coastal erosion has played its part, but concrete piers have been erected to prevent further destruction.

The ruins are haunted by the ghost of a Viking called Olaf who was badly wounded in a raid and nursed back to health by the priory monks. He stayed on and joined their community, but soon the marauding Vikings were back, and Olaf's brother was with them. He was killed in the fighting and Olaf was said to be so heartbroken that he died soon afterwards. Now his ghost can be seen looking wistfully out to sea, gazing back towards his homeland.

Tynemouth Priory and Castle, North Pier, Tynemouth, Tyne and Wear, NE30 4BZ; Tel: 0191 257 1090; Website: www.english-heritage.org.uk. Open daily 24 March–30 September.

There is no parking on site, but the town car park is nearby. Many special events take place at the castle, including Twilight Tours where guides in medieval costume invite you to take a tour of the castle and priory and learn something of the myths and legends of this area.

DEREK'S TIP

If you decide that you will use the home-made variety of ouija board, i.e. an upturned glass with letters and numbers placed around the edge of a table, the wearing of simple cotton gloves will eradicate any doubt that somebody is pushing the glass. With gloves, if an attempt is made, either consciously or unconsciously, to push the glass, then that person's fingertip will slide over its base.

Tyneside Cinema

Tyneside Cinema, as it is known today, opened as the Bijou News-Reel Cinema on 1 February 1937. The News Theatre building which houses it stands at the north-eastern edge of a site occupied as early as 1267 by Franciscans, or grey friars. Their monastery was a spiritual home to which many people flocked, hence the street upon which it stood being called Pilgrim Street. The entry lane which the box office entrance currently opens onto is called High Friar Lane. After Henry VIII suppressed the monasteries in 1539, the land was granted to the Earl of Essex. Shortly afterwards, the monastery was razed to the ground.

The next building to stand on the site was the Newe House, a mansion used by General Leven as his headquarters during the Civil War. Charles I was held there for 10 months until he was handed over to the Parliamentarians in 1647. The building in which the Tyneside Cinema is located is called the Newe House to this day, and this name can be seen above the Pilgrim Street entrance.

The Tyneside Cinema has a rich and varied history of ghostly sightings. In 1996 a mysterious monk was spotted simply standing in an office corridor, and when staff, thinking that he was a lost member of the public, asked if they could help, he simply disappeared. The cinema auditoria have also been places where strange things happen regularly. In 2005, two members of staff on different levels of an auditorium noticed a hunched figure sitting in the stalls area of the Classic cinema screen. It would not respond to them and disappeared into thin air...

In the early 1990s the cinema's cleaning team refused to come back due to paranormal activity and sightings in the Electra, which is the Tyneside's second screen. Almost every morning a single seat would be set in the 'down' position until the cleaners approached it.

Other strange experiences have ranged from staff names being called out to lights being turned on when nobody was there to do it and the mysterious presence felt by a medium at a late-night vigil in 2003 – at the very same spot where the monk was seen in 1996.

Tyneside Cinema, 10 Pilgrim Street, Newcastle upon Tyne, NE1 6QG; Tel: 0191 232 8289; Fax: 0191 221 0535; Website: www.tynecine.org

DEREK'S TIP

Remember that spirit people deserve the same respect that you would give a person living on Earth. It is ludicrous to expect a spirit person to respond to verbal abuse, for example. If you were that spirit person, would you respond to a person who treated you with respect or a person who used foul language and insults?

Whitby Abbey

Whitby Abbey is situated on a cliff overlooking the town and harbour. It dates back to the seventh century when Oswy, King of Northumbria, sent a princess named Hilda to found an abbey. She did so in 657 on the site of a former Roman signal station. She is now known as St Hilda and the abbey contains a shrine to her. The religious community, housing both women and men, became a busy cosmopolitan centre. It was destroyed during a Viking invasion in 867, but rebuilt by the Normans in the late 1070s. Following the Dissolution of the Monasteries in the sixteenth century, it became the property of the Cholmley family, who plundered it for building materials for a mansion.

Today the ruined abbey is a stark and beautiful place. It is Whitby's most popular attraction, but it has an eerie reputation. St Hilda herself is said to haunt the ruins. Her ghost, dressed in a shroud, has been sighted in one of the windows.

The other ghost haunting the abbey is also believed to be a nun, Constance de Beverley. She fell in love with a knight named Marmion and broke her vow of chastity. As a punishment she was bricked up in a cell and left to die. She is said to appear on the steps leading to the dungeons and to plead for her release.

Ghostly voices can also be heard at the abbey on the old Christmas Day, 6 January, when a phantom choir is said to sing in the ruins.

Whitby Abbey, Whitby, North Yorkshire, YO22 4JT; Tel: (01947) 603568; Website: www.english-heritage.co.uk. Open daily.

DEREK'S TIP

Don't rush things. Patience is required, as spirit people are not performers who just turn on and turn off, appearing on demand. If they are prepared to make themselves known, they will do it in their own good time. Always remember to thank them for their efforts.

Winter's Gibbet

Winter's Gibbet stands on a wild moorland road above the village of Elsdon in Northumberland, a severed head still swinging from it. The head is a fibre-glass one. It is a grisly memorial to William Winter, the last man in England to be gibbeted.

Winter was a gypsy and noted criminal. In 1791 he was charged with the brutal murder of an old woman, Margaret Crozier, who lived in a tower at Raw Pele, just north of Elsdon, and was reputed to have a secret hoard of money. He and the two women arrested with him, Jane and Eleanor Clark, claimed they had robbed the old lady but not killed her. However, evidence given by a shepherd boy, Robert Hindmarsh, condemned them all and they were hanged in Newcastle. The women's bodies were then sent to the surgeons' hall for dissection, but Winter's was hung on a gibbet at Whiskershields Common. It remained there for months, until the clothes had rotted away, then it was cut down and the bones scattered.

In Northumberland a gibbet is known as a stob and it was believed that rubbing slivers of wood from one on the gums would cure toothache. Bit by bit, pieces were taken off the original gibbet and finally it decayed completely. Around 1867 Sir Walter Travelyan of Wallington ordered a replica with a wooden body to be erected on his land. The body was often used as target practice and eventually only the head remained. Even that was frequently stolen and in 1998 the entire gibbet disappeared for a while. A joker left a miniature one in its place with a sign proclaiming that it would soon grow, given the current amount of rain!

Though Winter's body has long gone from the gibbet, it is said that the sound of rattling bones can often be heard there, especially on stormy nights, and that the ghosts of Winter and Jane and Eleanor Clark can been seen running from the old tower at Raw Pele.

Winter's Gibbet, Elsdon, Nr Otterburn, Northumberland

DEREK'S TIP

When researching a building where people have lived, do your best to ascertain high and low points in their lives, i.e. dates of birth, dates of passings, memorable events, etc. Times of great emotion imbue the fabric of a building with higher levels of residual energy, therefore it is on the anniversaries of these times that it is more likely that a spirit person will appear or that you will experience paranormal activity.

Ye Olde Black Boy

Ye Olde Black Boy is a traditional public house in Hull's old town. It dates back to 1720, when it was a pipe shop. Later it served as a coffee shop and a brothel before finally opening as a pub in the 1930s. It is well known for its real ales, ciders and fruit wines. It is thought that the name refers to a Moroccan boy who worked there in the 1730s, when it was a coffee shop.

There have been many rumours of ghosts in the pub. Bottles of malt whisky have apparently jumped off shelves by themselves and a pair of spectral hands has reached out from the panelled walls to grab customers round the neck!

Ye Olde Black Boy, 150 High Street, Hull, East Yorkshire, HU1 1PS; Tel: (01482) 326516. Live music on Thursday nights. Function room available free of charge.

Ye Olde Man and Scythe Inn

Ye Olde Man and Scythe Inn in Bolton is the fourth oldest public house in England. The vaulted cellar dates back to 1251, while the rest was rebuilt in 1636.

The pub saw dramatic times during the Civil War. In the Massacre of Bolton in 1644 between 100 and 500 soldiers and civilians were killed, mainly in the centre of town, in front of the pub. Horses were used to kill the soldiers. Then after the war, on 15 October 1651, the Royalist Earl of Derby, James Stanley, whose family had originally owned the pub, was beheaded outside it for his part in the war. The chair he sat in before he was taken outside is still in the pub today and some say that the Earl is still around as well.

Other ghosts are also believed to haunt the pub and many different paranormal phenomena have been experienced there. One woman once left her seat to find her hands covered in blood. The barman believed it had dripped through the ceiling, but there was no blood to be seen there at the time.

Ye Olde Man and Scythe Inn, 6–8 Churchgate, Bolton, Lancashire, BL1 1HL; Tel: (01204) 527267; Website: www.manandscythe.co.uk

The pub serves both traditional Lancashire food and more exotic dishes. The execution of the Earl of Derby is re-enacted every 15 October.

THE MIDLANDS

Abbey Pumping Station, Leicester

The Alexandra Theatre, Birmingham

Brownsover Hall Hotel, Warwickshire

The Castle Hotel, Castleton

Edgehill Battlefield, Warwickshire

Edwards No. 8 Rock Club, Birmingham

The Grail Court Hotel, Burton-on-Trent

The Griffin Inn, Nuneaton

Ladybower Reservoir, Derbyshire

The Parade Shopping Centre, Shrewsbury

The Red Lion, Wirksworth

The Shire Hall Gallery, Stafford

Shrewsbury Museum and Art Gallery

Shrewsbury Railway Station

The Shropshire Union Canal

Stafford Superbowl

Weston Hall, Staffs.

Winnats Pass, Derbyshire

I think that I may have mentioned in my book *Ghost Hunting with Derek Acorah* that Mr Richard Felix would argue that his home town of Derby is the most haunted place in the country. He refers to it as 'the dead centre of England'! There are others, however, who would argue that point.

The Midlands covers a huge area of central England where so much of our country's history is entrenched. From the Civil War right through to the Industrial Revolution and beyond, the Midlands was at the heart of events. Now that heart of England continues to beat with supernatural happenings that defy logical explanation.

Abbey Pumping Station

Abbey Pumping Station, next to the National Space Centre in Leicester, is a museum of science and technology. Opened in 1891, it originally pumped Leicester's sewage to the treatment works at Beaumont Leys. It closed in 1964, but was preserved because of the magnificent Victorian engineering on display in the four beam steam engines that were used to pump the sewage. Three of these have been restored to working condition. The pumping station now holds special steam events and has exhibitions on light and optics, historic transport and public health.

There have been many unexplained events at the pumping house, mostly around the engine house. Items have been moved around and strange noises have often been heard, particularly late at night when the museum is about to be locked up. The disturbances are supposed to be due to the ghost of an engineer who worked at the pumping station in the nineteenth century. He died there in 1890, when he fell over 50 ft from the top balcony down into the engine room. His friends commemorated him with an inscription on the basement wall.

Abbey Pumping Station, Corporation Road, Abbey Lane, Leicester, LE4 5PX; Tel: 0116 299 5111

Open February–November Saturday–Wednesday and certain Thursdays and Fridays during the school holidays. Open December–January for special events and private hire.

DEREK'S TIP

If nothing happens on your first investigation, do not be too disappointed. Spirit people are not performers and will only appear if and when they want to. Just because you have had no success on one investigation does not mean that you will fail on others.

The Alexandra Theatre, Birmingham

The Alexandra Theatre in the heart of Birmingham is a well-established theatre which offers a variety of pre- and post-West End productions, opera, ballet, musical theatre and other live performances. It dates back to Edwardian times and seats over 1,300 people. It is the home of the D'Oyly Carte Opera Company, formed by Richard D'Oyly in 1871, which performs the works of Gilbert and Sullivan. Playbox Theatre, one of the leading theatre organizations for young people, also performs there.

The theatre is reputed to be haunted by the ghost of a former manager, Leon Salberg, who ran the theatre in the 1930s. His footsteps can be heard in one of the offices and though he has not been seen, his presence can be felt around the theatre, especially in the stalls.

One ghostly figure which has been seen in the theatre is that of a woman in grey. It is believed that she is a former wardrobe mistress who died unexpectedly one night at the theatre.

The Alexandra Theatre, Station Street, Birmingham B5 4DS; Tel: 0870 607 7544 (tickets/info); 0121 643 3168 (group bookings)

Brownsover Hall Hotel

Brownsover Hall Hotel, near Rugby, is a Victorian Gothic mansion designed by Sir George Gilbert Scott and set in seven acres of garden and woodland. It was formerly the home of the Boughton-Leigh family. In Elizabethan times, one member of the family, known as 'One-Handed Boughton' because his hand had been severed, used to drive round the estate in a coach and six. After he died, his ghost continued to do so. By 1755 the family had had enough of it and called in a team of 12 clergymen to carry out an exorcism. The spirit was persuaded to enter a bottle, which was sealed up and thrown into a lake in the grounds. There it remained until the 1880s, when it was found by a fisherman and returned to the family. After that a phantom coach and six began to be heard once more in the grounds.

In 1939 a research establishment was set up in the hall under the direction of Sir Frank Whittle, father of the modern jet engine. The night watchmen and cleaners soon realized the place was haunted, as they often heard voices and footsteps when the building was empty, as well as the sound of horses' hooves and carriage wheels on the drive. These phenomena have all continued to this day and the hotel staff have grown so used to them that they have become almost blasé about them!

Brownsover Hall Hotel, Brownsover Lane, Old Brownsover, Nr Rugby, Warwickshire, CV21 1HU; Tel: (01788) 56100

The Castle Hotel

The seventeenth-century Castle Hotel is a former coaching inn in Castleton, an old lead-mining village in the Peak District. The village is the venue for the traditional Garland or Oak Apple Day ceremony which takes place every 29 May to celebrate spring. Although it is based on a pagan festival, in the seventeenth century it became associated with the story of Charles II hiding in an oak tree to avoid Cromwell's soldiers. During the celebration 'King Charles' and his 'lady' ride through the village from pub to pub carrying a three-foot high garland of flowers and oak leaves. Finally they place the garland on the church tower.

The village is also known for Blue John, a rare banded form of fluorospar, which is mined nearby and used for a variety of decorative purposes. The Castle Hotel itself is said to be haunted by four ghosts. One of Charles II's soldiers only appears from the knees upwards, but the other ghosts can be seen in their entirety. An elderly housekeeper still monitors the premises, and Cooper, a man in a pinstriped suit, still sneaks in by a former side entrance so that his wife won't catch him drinking. There is also a lady in grey called Rose, though her history is unclear. Some say she is a jilted bride, others that she is a former chambermaid.

The Castle Hotel, Castle Street, Castleton, Derbyshire, S33 8WG; Tel: (01433) 620578; Fax: (01433) 622902

The Blue John Cavern, Tel: (01433) 620638/620642. Open daily except Christmas.

Edgehill Battlefield

The Battle of Edgehill, or Kineton Fight as it was sometimes known, was the first major battle of the Civil War. It took place on 23 October 1642. King Charles I had set out from Shrewsbury for London and the government sent Robert Devereux, Earl of Essex, the Parliamentarian Lord General, to intercept him. The two armies, both 15,000 strong, met halfway and fought in open fields between the villages of Radway and Kineton in Warwickshire.

This was intended to be the one great battle to decide the war. It started around 2 o'clock in the afternoon and went on until night-fall, but ended in an inconclusive draw. Around 1,000 men were killed and 2–3,000 wounded. The bodies were looted and left. The Earl of Essex withdrew to the garrison at Warwick and the Royalists were left in command of the road to London.

Today the battlefield is largely agricultural land. Most is owned by the Ministry of Defence. A military depot was built there in the late 1940s.

The site is believed to be one of the most haunted in Warwickshire. Just a month after the battle, local shepherds heard the sound of drums and then saw what they thought was another battle being fought, but suddenly the scene vanished into thin air. So many similar tales were reported that the printer Thomas Jackson published them in 1643. The king himself was intrigued and sent six senior statesmen to revisit the site. They too witnessed an eerie re-enactment of the battle and three of them recognized men they knew to be dead.

Sightings of the armies are less frequent now, but the thundering hooves of the cavalry charges and the cries of the wounded are still heard at night, particularly around the anniversary of the battle.

Edgehill, between Radway and Kineton, Warwickshire

A monument stands in memory of those who died in the battle.

DEREK'S TIP

If you are tempted to try to invoke spirit people without the presence of a trained medium, do ensure that you offer up a prayer of self-protection first.

Edwards No. 8 Rock Club

Edwards No. 8 Rock Club in Birmingham city centre was once a hospital for skin and rare diseases, with a mortuary on the top floor. Now it offers a range of rock music throughout the week and live music on Fridays, Saturdays and Sundays. Food is also available and there is a pub downstairs.

A variety of strange phenomena have occurred at the club, including tools and other utensils being moved, lifted into the air and used to make noises. Shortly after the present manager arrived the till started ringing frantically on its own and then suddenly stopped. After a while the manager decided to take matters in hand. Feeling slightly foolish, he talked to an empty room, explaining his plans for the club. After that, things calmed down. Some staff still won't go into 'cold' areas such as the back room and places where bottles are stored, though, as they feel they are sinking into the floor!

When I visited the club in November last year I realized that spirit people were dropping by in visitation. They may have been hospital staff checking out their former workplace or patients who remembered the kindness and care they had experienced there, but either way they were enjoying the lively atmosphere and the music!

Edwards No. 8 Rock Club, Lower Severn Street, Birmingham B1 1BL; Tel: 0121 643 5835

The Grail Court Hotel

The Grail Court Hotel in the centre of Burton-on-Trent is part of a Grade II listed building and has its own licensed bar and restaurant, Arthur's, and nightclub, Merlin's.

The current owners purchased the hotel around five years ago as a derelict building. All the previous owners had gone bankrupt within two years of owning the property. The last had left a year before. Since then the building had been visited by bailiffs and squatters and rendered virtually uninhabitable. Many late nights had to be spent rebuilding the hotel.

One night two members of staff were working in the cellar. It was a Sunday and there was no one else in the building, which was completely locked up. Directly above them, in the restaurant, they suddenly heard small footsteps running to and fro and the sound of children giggling. They dropped everything and ran upstairs, thinking someone had got into the restaurant, but everything was in darkness and still locked up. Both laughed and returned to their work in the cellar, but minutes later they heard a door slam, then more footsteps and laughter. This time they did not investigate, but left in something of a hurry.

Since then many hotel guests have expressed delight at the charming little girl in a white nightdress who has run past them giggling. Some people have even been kept awake at night by the sound of a little girl playing in the corridors, but there have been no children staying in the hotel at the time.

Even more disturbing have been the red crayon marks found in the bath in room 21. This room faces onto the main road junction and many people have seen the face of a young girl peering out of the window when no guests have been staying in the room. The crayon appears at least once a week.

Recently two BBC researchers stayed in that room. They checked the bath before retiring at about 11 p.m. and there was no crayon to be seen. At 12.30 a.m. they were woken by the sound of a girl giggling outside the room. They went out to investigate but found no one there and returned to bed. A little later they were woken by more giggles and found that their bedroom curtains were now open, as though someone had drawn them back to look out of the window. When they checked the bath, red crayon lines had appeared on the bottom of it. They got back into bed and then the phone rang. They picked it up, but no one was there. This happened three times. Yet at the time the phone was not working, due to an internal line fault. The hotel manager had tested it himself that day and the line was completely dead.

The Grail Court Hotel is also haunted by many other ghosts. A coachman dressed in a long flowing cape wanders around outside the building and has even been caught several times on CCTV. 'John the Barrelman' hides in the cellar and is often heard banging about. The Avalon Suite, which was once three small cottages and before that Civil War stables, is one of the most haunted parts of the hotel. A businesswoman staying there was once surprised to see a group of ghosts standing around a coffin.

The Grail Court Hotel, Station Street, Burton-on-Trent, Staffordshire, DE14 1BN; Tel: (01283) 741155; Fax: (01283) 741166

The Grail Court Hotel is now part of Burton Ghost Walks. Website: www.burtonghosts.co.uk.

The Griffin Inn

The Griffin Inn at Griff, Nuneaton, is a historic pub which was first given a victualling licence in 1654 in order to supply ale to the miners in the shallow bell pits and diggings of the surrounding area.

For years there have been mysterious knockings in the pub and compressed air cylinders and beer taps have been inexplicably turned off. Even the installation of a modern alarm system has made no difference. A collection of old locks on a shelf in the lounge has been found scattered over the floor in the morning and once a one-armed bandit that was switched off at the mains suddenly gave out a jackpot of £70.

It is believed that the ghost is that of a Victorian woman. One of the landlords and his partner once witnessed an old lady in black sitting on the end of their bed, and in 1995 the licensee was woken by his dog barking furiously and saw a tall woman wearing a veil over her face standing in his bedroom. As soon as he switched on the light, she disappeared.

The Griffin Inn, Coventry Rd, Griff, Nuneaton, Warwickshire, CV10 7PJ; Tel: 024 7631 1870. Serves food.

Ladybower Reservoir

Ladybower Reservoir in Derbyshire is the largest of a chain of three reservoirs known as the Peakland Lake District. It is situated in the Peak District National Park and provides drinking water for the north and east Midlands. Construction began in 1935 and was completed ten years later. It entailed the flooding of two villages, Ashopton and Derwent. At the time Ladybower was the largest reservoir in the country.

The 'Dambuster' squadron of the RAF used the Derwent reservoirs during the Second World War to test the 'bouncing bomb' and to practise for their famous raid on the Ruhr dams. A ghostly Lancaster Bomber has since been seen in the area by several witnesses. This may be 'Vicky the Vicious Virgin' which crashed during a routine training flight on 18 May 1945, killing all six of the crew.

A United States Air Force Dakota has also been seen since the war. This may be the ghost of a Dakota which crashed on 24 July 1945 in almost the same spot, killing all eight on board.

The area has also been the focus for strange lights in the sky, which may be related to the phantom planes. Over the years many people have contacted the police to report an aircrash and yet the mountain rescue service has found nothing. Once a man distinctly saw a plane descending in a fireball, but no wreckage was ever found. Sometimes the sound of a crashing plane has been heard but nothing has been seen.

Ladybower Reservoir is accessible from the A57 from Glossop or Sheffield. The visitor centre is off the A57, west of Sheffield, over Ashopton viaduct adjacent to the reservoir.

Upper Derwent Visitor Centre, Fairholmes, Derwent, Sheffield, S30 2AQ; Tel: (01433) 651261.

Open daily from Easter to the end of October and winter weekends. There is a small shop, toilets, car park and snack bar. Cycles are available for hire.

DEREK'S TIP

If your group is planning to split up in order to conduct lone vigils, do make sure that everybody is equipped with some form of communication, i.e. walkie-talkie or mobile phone, and do make sure that as many people as possible carry a camera of sorts.

The Parade Shopping Centre

The Parade Shopping Centre is in the heart of medieval Shrewsbury, at the top of Pride Hill. It is situated on two floors in a Grade II listed building which was completed in 1826 and has a terrace café overlooking the River Severn.

The building used to be the Royal Salop Infirmary and it is said that some of the hospital staff are still there taking care of things.

New tenants in the shops usually experience strange events for the first year or so and then things settle down as they are accepted by 'Matron'! She is the ghost of a hospital matron of the 1920s. In life she was organized and efficient and it seems that she is still intent on keeping things in order. One man once spent two hours putting up posters on the ceiling of his collectable toy and model shop only to find when he unlocked the shop the next morning that they were in rows on the floor. On another occasion plaques and trophies that had been hung haphazardly on the wall were placed above the fireplace in a straight line. Other tenants have also found that stock items left in a mess will be arranged neatly in rows, while other things are moved round or thrown off shelves or walls. Even furniture is moved about and doors suddenly close on their own. However, Matron is never intimidating – just a stickler for tidiness! She also has a compassionate side. When the building was still a hospital it was said that she used to appear at the foot of dying people's beds in order to help them over to the next world.

The shopping centre is also said to be haunted by a young nurse who became pregnant and committed suicide by hanging herself there.

The Parade Shopping Centre, St Mary's Place, Shrewsbury, Shropshire, SY1 1DL; Tel: (01743) 343178. There is a car park next to the shopping centre.

DEREK'S TIP

If lone vigils are undertaken, ensure that people are in rooms far enough apart. Noises carry and are intensified at night. You do not want to confuse the footsteps or movements of another investigator with those of any possible spirit presence.

The Red Lion

The Red Lion in Wirksworth, near the Peak District National Park, is a hospitable former coaching inn providing accommodation, meals and roaring log fires. It was rebuilt in the eighteenth century, but may date to medieval times.

The area was known for lead mining as far back as Roman times. The industry peaked between 1600 and 1780, then declined dramatically in the late nineteenth century, especially after lead ore was discovered at Broken Hill in Australia, and many mines were closed. Limestone quarrying largely took its place as the local industry until the 1920s, when mechanization was introduced. Now the Peak District is a highly popular tourist destination and Wirksworth itself has won the prestigious Europa Nostra Award for architectural conservation.

The Red Lion is haunted by the ghost of a coachman. One day he was trying to manoeuvre his coach through the archway when the horses suddenly bolted and, taken by surprise, he was decapitated. Now his headless figure can be seen wandering the premises.

The Red Lion, Market Place, Wirksworth, Derbyshire, DE4 4ET; Tel: (01629) 822214; Website: www.redlionwirksworth.co.uk

The Shire Hall Gallery

The Shire Hall Gallery in Stafford is situated in a Grade II listed building formerly used as the Crown Court. The library and Tourist Information Centre have recently moved into the same building. The gallery features paintings, drawings and prints by Staffordshire artists.

The ghost said to walk the area is known as Claude. His territory extends from the Shire Hall Gallery through the library and down to the Tourist Information Centre. Nothing is known of his origins, however, and he remains a mystery.

The Shire Hall Gallery, Library and Tourist Information Centre, Market Square, Stafford, ST16 2LD; Tel: (01785) 278345; Fax: (01785) 278599; Website: www.staffordshire.gov.uk/sams. Open every day. There is a café and shop.

Shrewsbury Museum and Art Gallery

Shrewsbury Museum and Art Gallery are housed in a traditional timber-framed Tudor warehouse and town house. The museum specializes in archaeology, natural history, geology, costume and local history. The archaeology section includes pieces from as early as 12,000 BC, while the local history display features excavation material from Roman Wroxeter. As well as the permanent displays, the museum holds many temporary exhibitions.

Two ghosts walk the museum and art gallery. One is a well-dressed lady who has been seen resting upon a four-poster bed which is now on display and also at the bed's original location in the building. The other ghost is from the same period, judging by his costume, but does not appear to have any connection with the lady. He is said to have appeared long before she did and to have haunted the property when it was still a private home.

Shrewsbury Museum and Art Gallery, Rowley's House, Barker Street, Shrewsbury, Shropshire, SY1 1QH; Tel: (01743) 361196; Fax: (01743) 358411

Shrewsbury Railway Station

In the heyday of the railways Shrewsbury station was the gateway to Wales and the north. Now it remains an important cross-country junction for both passengers and freight.

One former passenger has not moved on since 1887, however. He is a Shrewsbury councillor who had just arrived at the station when he was killed by a falling roof, which also crushed his carriage and injured his horse. Since then he has been seen either standing or sitting near the ramp entrance from Castle Street.

Shrewsbury Railway Station, Castle Foregate, Shrewsbury, Shropshire, SY1 2DQ; Tel: 0845 6061 660 (customer services)

DEREK'S TIP

I can recommend the use of pendulums in investigations, especially those constructed of quartz crystal. When close to a spirit energy, pendulums have been known to swing or spin. The closer you go to that energy source, the more rapid the movement of the pendulum.

The Shropshire Union Canal

The Shropshire Union Canal, or 'Shroppie', runs for 67 miles from Ellesmere Port near Liverpool to Autherley Junction near Wolverhampton. It was formed in 1846, when there was an amalgamation of several different canals and waterway companies. From the mid-nineteenth century onwards railways began to take over the transport of freight and in the decades following the First World War parts of the Shropshire Union were closed, but in the 1960s there was a revival of interest in the canal network and today the Shropshire Union Canal is a very important part of the pleasure boat network.

It is also one of Britain's most haunted canals. At the old Northgate in Chester a Roman centurion has been seen guarding the entrance to the city. An American pilot who crashed during the Second World War has been seen at Little Onn, near Church Eaton in Staffordshire. At Betton Cutting, near Market Drayton, ghostly shrieking has been heard, while just beyond Market Drayton, at Tyrley middle lock, it is said that if you arrive in the middle of the night the resident ghost will close the lock gates behind you.

Probably the best-known phantom on the Shropshire Union, however, appears at the lovely hamlet of Norbury Junction. At this point the canal descends into the dark Grub Street cutting. The High Bridge above this, the double-arched Bridge 39, is supposedly haunted by a black shaggy-coated or even simian creature said to be the ghost of a boatman who drowned there in the nineteenth century. He is known locally as 'the Monkey Man'.

Stafford Superbowl

The Stafford Superbowl is a highly popular venue for ten pin bowling, pool and Quasar, but some claim the building is never really empty, even when there is no one there! Odd mumbling has often been heard there, as if several people are talking quietly amongst themselves. One senior mechanic felt the sound was following him from lane to lane and was so frightened that he could not continue preparing the bowling lanes and had to go to the main entrance and wait until someone else arrived.

There have been a variety of other strange incidents. A hanging man has been seen by a cleaner in Quasar, lights have exploded inexplicably in the pool room and the telephone has malfunctioned on many occasions.

The building stands on the site of the former infirmary's morgue, which may have something to do with the paranormal phenomena experienced there.

Stafford Superbowl, Greyfriars Place, Stafford, ST16 2SD; Tel: (01785) 256050; Website: www.megabowl.co.uk. Open every day, 6 p.m.–12 p.m.

Weston Hall

Weston Hall is a hotel and restaurant with an award-winning garden. It was built in the sixteenth century and for several years after 1898 was used as a lunatic asylum for paupers, taking overspill patients from St George's County Asylum in Stafford. In the Second World War it was used as a barracks by the army and later became private flats before being turned into a hotel.

A Grey Lady is said to walk the hall and many strange events have been reported in the house and grounds. Within a few days of opening in September 1996, hotel staff found that the bar area had been mysteriously cleaned each morning, even though no cleaning staff had been in and the alarm system had been working throughout the night.

Staff have also heard women's voices talking in empty rooms and have been called by name when they were alone in the building. Mysterious piano music has also been heard and in the early hours of the morning carriages, horses and footmen have been heard on the gravel outside – except that there is no longer any gravel there…

Weston Hall, Weston Bank, Weston, Nr Stafford, ST18 0BA; Tel: (01889) 271700

Winnats Pass

Winnats Pass is a steep narrow limestone gorge which leads into the village of Castleton in Derbyshire. At its foot, 600 feet below ground, is Speedwell Cavern, one of four deep caverns in the area. There is also an underground canal, which was formed when a lead miners' tunnel flooded. It is 2,625 feet long and ends in a cavern known as the Bottomless Pit, because 40,000 tons of rubble were dumped into it without changing the water level.

The pass itself is said to be haunted by two young lovers, Alan (or alternatively Henry) and Clara. Their parents did not approve of their relationship, but at the time, the mid-eighteenth century, anyone could get married in the Peak Forest, day or night. The young couple decided to elope, but as they were going through Winnats Pass on their way to the forest, they were robbed and murdered by three lead miners. Their bodies were found years later, lying together in a shallow grave.

The miners were never caught, but the story runs that in one way or another they were all punished for their crime: one hanged himself, one was killed in a rockfall and one went mad.

To this day it is said that the voices of the young lovers can be heard crying for mercy as the wind whistles through Winnats Pass.

Winnats Pass, Castleton, Derbyshire

Speedwell Cavern, Castleton, Derbyshire; Tel: (01433) 620512; Fax: (01433) 621888. Open daily apart from Christmas Day.

DEREK'S TIP

Give each investigator the opportunity to call out to the spirit world. Whilst one person's voice vibration may fail to attract the attention of spirit entities, another person's voice may just be appealing enough to generate activity. Personalities are carried on voice vibrations and like attracts like – it is spiritual law. A spirit person may respond to a certain personality type because they have similar traits, whereas they will ignore another.

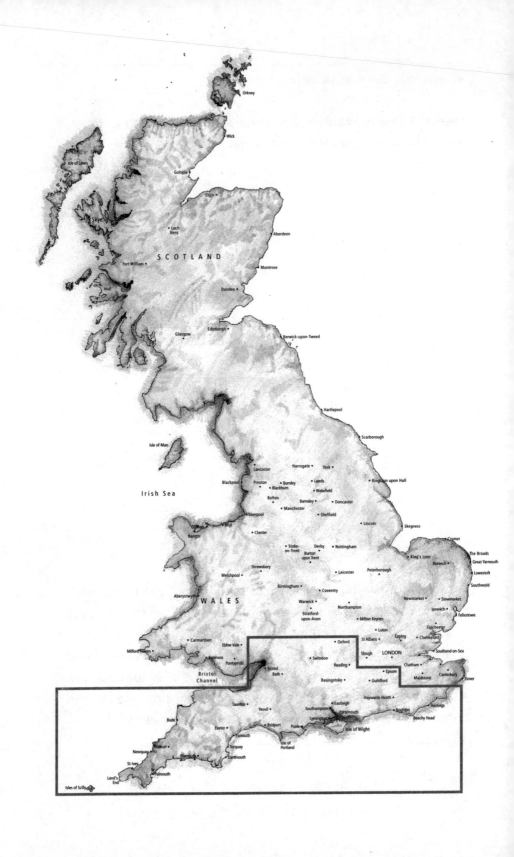

SOUTHERN ENGLAND

The ABC Cinema, Plymouth

The Angel Hotel, Lymington

Battle Abbey, East Sussex

The Brushmaker's Arms, Hampshire

Corfe Castle, Dorset

Dimbola Lodge Museum, Isle of Wight

Dozmary Pool, Bodmin Moor

Dunster Castle, Somerset

The Farringford Hotel, Isle of Wight

The George Hotel, Crawley

Hastings Castle, East Sussex

The Hill House, Ross-on-Wye

The Holt Hotel, Oxfordshire

The New Inn, Pembridge

Newquay, Cornwall

Nunney, Somerset

Okehampton Castle, Devon

Pevensey Castle, East Sussex

The Royal Victoria Country Park, Southampton

Theatre Royal Winchester

Tintagel Castle, Cornwall

The Trout Inn, Oxford

Westbury Swimming Pool, Wilts.

Yeovil Railway Station Buffet, Somerset

From Oxfordshire down to the southern coast of England and beyond to the Isle of Wight, west to Cornwall and up through Devon and Somerset, this section of the United Kingdom is filled with mysticism and legends of old. From the pretty villages of the Isle of Wight to the brooding moors of Exmoor, Dartmoor and Bodmin, the area holds stories of ghostly happenings and events that can only be classified as paranormal.

My own favourite spot in this part of the world is Somerset, particularly the wonderful town of Glastonbury. I could walk for hours in the ancient dignity and grace of the ruined Glastonbury Abbey, absorbing an atmosphere that exists nowhere else on Earth. To walk up the Tor to the tower dedicated to St Michael and look out over the Vale of Avalon is an incomparable experience.

The ABC Cinema, Plymouth

The ABC Cinema in Plymouth is one of the few buildings that were left standing in the town after the heavy bombing of the Second World War. It stands on the site of the original Theatre Royal, which burned down in the early 1900s.

Over the years there have been numerous reports of a presence within the cinema. These have mainly been centred around Screen 2. The majority have involved the sighting of a female figure dressed in a red skirt and jacket. She has been seen by both employees and customers, but when the lights go on, she is not there. The sightings apparently increase when a horror film in shown and the complex has had problems with the sound system, though it is not known whether these are related.

The haunting is thought to be connected to the days when the Theatre Royal was Plymouth's major theatre and an actress committed suicide there by hanging herself in her dressing room.

Torbay Investigators of the Paranormal (TIP) recently conducted two overnight investigations at the cinema and recorded light orbs and irregular magnetic fields. A local medium who was with them picked up the name 'Winnie' or 'Minnie'. Further investigations are scheduled with a Plymouth group called Magic2K.

The ABC Cinema, Derry's Cross, Plymouth, Devon, PL1 2SW; Tel: (01752) 663300

The Angel Hotel

Lymington is a small market town on the estuary of the Boldre river. Its dockyards once provided more ships to the Royal Navy than Portsmouth, but now there are just a few slipways left and the harbour is mainly used by private yachts and the Isle of Wight ferry.

The thirteenth-century Angel Hotel was the favourite inn of the shipbuilders and sailors of the town. It was once known as the George, but the name was changed around 1768, possibly for political reasons, as a George was on the throne at the time.

At that time the hotel was a coaching inn and local people would often gather to watch the Royal Mail coach leave for Southampton and London. One of hotel's ghosts is that of a coachman. He can often be seen in the early morning standing at the kitchen window looking out into the yard as though keeping watch over the loading of the Royal Mails.

The hotel is also haunted by a tall grey-haired man in a naval-style coat with brass buttons fastened up to the neck. He has been seen on many occasions, usually late at night. He may be the ghost of an officer who stayed at the hotel the night before he was due to appear in court. He never made it to the courtroom because he committed suicide in the hotel bedroom first.

The second floor of the hotel is haunted by the ghost of a blonde girl dressed in white, though very little is known about her.

In the 1960s, a couple staying in one of the rooms adjoining the old Assembly Hall heard a piano being played in the middle of the night. The next day they complained to the hotel manager about the noise, but he explained that the piano which had stood in the Assembly Hall had been so badly damaged that it had been taken away just the day before. The couple would not believe it until they were taken into the room and saw for themselves that there was no earthly piano there.

The Angel Hotel, 108 High Street, Lymington, Hampshire, SO41 9AP; Tel: (01590) 672050; Fax: (01590) 671661

DEREK'S TIP

It is pointless to shout and scream at every little noise. Put yourself in the place of the spirit person. If somebody standing next to you were suddenly to jump and yell out, what would you do? I am sure that you would beat a hasty retreat! And that is exactly what spirit people do when confronted with such behaviour.

Battle Abbey

Battle Abbey was built on the site of the famous Battle of Hastings, which took place when William of Normandy invaded Britain in 1066. The two armies did not actually fight at Hastings, but at a place north of the town, which is now named Battle. The Saxons occupied the higher ground and the battle raged inconclusively for several hours until the Normans pretended to flee and the Saxons broke ranks to pursue them, whereupon the Normans turned back and cut them down. King William later built an abbey on the site to atone for the loss of life during the conquest.

Some of the original abbey is still visible today, though parts were turned into a country house following the Dissolution of the Monasteries under Henry VIII. The parkland of the abbey includes the ground believed to be the site of the battle.

Several ghosts linger on there. In the huge Common House, constructed as a dining-room for visiting dignitaries, the ghosts of an elderly man in a brown monk's habit, a Norman knight and a young boy have been seen. Another knight is said to walk across the battlefield and one appears on horseback on 14 October, the anniversary of the battle. The ground also seems to bleed after a storm, though a more prosaic explanation for this is iron oxide in the soil.

In and around the grounds mysterious footsteps have been heard and on different occasions a lady in a red Elizabethan dress and another lady in grey have been seen. Horses' hooves have been heard by the magnificent arched gatehouse and people often feel uncomfortable there.

A black monk has been seen in several places, including the Guest House, Monks' Walk and outside the abbey. Even the ghost of King Harold has apparently put in an appearance on the anniversary of the battle, complete with an arrow jutting from his eye!

Battle Abbey, Battle, East Sussex, TN33 0AD; Tel: (01424) 773792; Fax: (01424) 775059; Website: www.english-heritage.org.uk. Open from the beginning of January to the end of March.

The Brushmaker's Arms

The Brushmaker's Arms is a traditional pub with a large garden. It got its name because in the past it served as a base for brushmakers in the Vale of Upham.

One regular guest was a brushmaker called Mr Chickett. He was famed for the quality of his brushes and reputed to make a very good living. Rumour also had it that he carried all his money with him and slept with it under his pillow. Inevitably one night when he was staying at the inn he was robbed and murdered. Ever since, his shadowy figure has been seen roaming the inn as though hunting for something – probably his lost fortune. Sometimes he cannot be seen but dogs seem to be aware of his presence.

The Brushmaker's Arms, Shoe Lane, Upham, Nr Winchester, Hants., SO32 1JJ; Tel: (01489) 860231. Food served. Folk music monthly on Thursday evenings.

Corfe Castle

The ruins of Corfe Castle stand on a hill off the A351 Wareham–Swanage road to the north-west of Corfe Castle village. A Roman fort once occupied this spot, then in the ninth century a wooden castle was built. It was rebuilt from stone in the eleventh century and became royal property from the time of William the Conqueror. In the thirteenth century King John greatly enhanced it with a new hall, chapel and outbuildings. Henry III later extended it with more walls, towers and gatehouses. At that time it was an important stronghold guarding a gap in the Purbeck Hills. In 1572 Elizabeth I sold it to her dancing master, Sir Christopher Hatton, and in 1635 it became the property of Sir John Bankes, the Lord Chief Justice.

During the Civil War the castle was besieged twice by Parliamentarians. In 1643, Lady Bankes, Sir John's widow, successfully defended it, but in February 1646, the treachery of an insider led to Parliamentarian troops entering the castle disguised as Royalist reinforcements. The castle fell and Parliament ordered it to be slighted, leaving it the ruin that can be seen today.

It is said that Corfe Castle was the inspiration for Kirrin Castle in Enid Blyton's Famous Five books.

Strange lights have been seen at the castle at night and it is said that they are carried by the ghosts of Civil War soldiers. A headless woman has been seen walking on the hill near the castle gateway.

Corfe Castle, The Square, Corfe Castle, Wareham, Dorset, BH20 5EZ; Tel: (01929) 481294 (general), (01929) 480609 (learning centre), (01929) 480921 (shop), (01929) 481332 (tea-room); Fax: (01929) 477067; E-mail: corfecastle@nationaltrust.org.uk; Website: www.nationaltrust.org.uk. Open daily, apart from 25 and 26 December. Parts of the grounds may be closed in high winds.

There is a visitor centre, Castle View, on the A351 north of the castle, which includes interactive displays and a schools room. Guided tours are often available. Free parking is available at Castle View.

The Swanage Railway operates a steam train service from the Norden Park and Ride just outside Corfe Castle to Swanage, stopping at the castle.

DEREK'S TIP

Compare notes with other investigative groups to establish whether you have made similar findings to them. The more similarities exist, the more likely it is that you have experienced paranormal activity.

Dimbola Lodge Museum

Dimbola Lodge at Freshwater on the Isle of Wight is the former home of the pioneering photographer Julia Margaret Cameron (1815–79). After living for many years in Ceylon, she moved to London on her husband Charles' retirement in 1848 and became part of Kensington's artistic community, which included the Poet Laureate Alfred, Lord Tennyson. In 1860, while visiting Tennyson at his home at Farringford House *(see page 132)*, she bought two adjacent cottages from a local fisherman, Jacob Long, linked them by means of a Gothic tower – which dominates the Freshwater skyline to this day – and named the new house Dimbola after her family's tea plantation in Ceylon. She lived there for the next 15 years and it was there that she was given a camera by her daughter and son-in-law and began her photographic career, converting the fowl-house into a studio and the coal-house into a dark room and producing over 3,000 photographs.

Her main interest was portraits and she produced some striking and definitive images of eminent Victorian writers, artists and scientists, including Tennyson, Darwin and Thackeray, who lived locally, and Lewis Carroll, Robert Browning, Edward Lear and Ellen Terry.

The Cameron family returned to Ceylon in 1875 and many years later Dimbola Lodge was again divided in two parts, named Dimbola and Cameron House. By 1993, Dimbola had become a private residence and holiday flats, and Cameron House was unoccupied and threatened with demolition. Fortunately the Julia Margaret Cameron Trust was able to buy first Cameron House and then Dimbola and restore the Lodge. It has since been Grade II listed and now houses a museum and galleries, a bookshop and a tea room specializing in vegetarian food. It hosts both historical and contemporary photographic exhibitions.

There was a major retrospective of Julia Margaret Cameron's work at the National Portrait Gallery, London, recently.

It is said that the photographer herself still haunts Dimbola Lodge wearing her favourite brown taffeta dress. People have reported a strange smell in the gift shop, which is supposed to be that of the chemicals that she used to fix her photographs. It is also said to appear when her favourite classical music is played in the tea room. Visitors have also reported seeing phantom maids on the stairs and other ghostly figures around the house and grounds.

Dimbola Lodge Museum, Terrace Lane, Freshwater Bay, Isle of Wight, PO40 9QE; Tel: (01983) 756814; Website: www.dimbola.co.uk

Dozmary Pool

Dozmary Pool, meaning 'Drop of Sea', is a moorland lake to the south of Bolventor on Bodmin Moor. According to legend it was bottomless and had a whirlpool in the centre and a tunnel connecting it to the sea, but in 1869 it dried up completely, which quashed that idea. However, it is still home to many tales of the supernatural.

It is claimed that Dozmary Pool is the lake into which Sir Bedivere threw King Arthur's sword Excalibur after the king was mortally wounded. The Lady of the Lake, guardian of Excalibur, reached up a hand and caught the sword, holding it aloft for a moment before drawing it beneath the water, where it remains to this day.

The site is also linked with local legends of a man called Jan Tregeagle. He was an early seventeenth-century magistrate famed for his cruelty. He was rumoured to have murdered his wife and children, sold his soul to the Devil and made his fortune by robbing an orphan of his estate. After his death some of the people he had swindled went to court to try to get back their land. At the end of the trial the judge was about to sum up when a final witness was called: Jan Treageagle himself. The court laughed, but was horrified when a shadowy figure began to appear in the witness box. Undeterred, the judge calmly questioned the ghost, who testified that he had indeed swindled the defendants.

After the trial, Jan was reluctant to go back to hell and the vicar decided that he should be kept busy in the area instead. He was set to emptying Dozmary Pool with a leaking limpet shell while the dogs of hell watched over him, waiting to drag him back to hell if he stopped working. After a while he couldn't stand it any longer and escaped, only to be set other impossible tasks. He ended up at Porthcurno Cove, sweeping the sand to the Mill Bay every day only to see the tide turn and sweep it all back again. It is said that he is still there and his screams of frustration can be heard on the howling wind.

Dozmary Pool lies two miles from Jamaica Inn, off a minor road from the A30.

DEREK'S TIP

Spirits cannot harm the living. There is nothing to be frightened of. As an experienced medium, when I allow a spirit entity to draw close to my aura I am channelling that person's personality and emotions. I am not possessed. Some spirits may not enter the atmosphere if they sense that you are scared, as they will have no wish to frighten you.

Dunster Castle

Dunster Castle, near Minehead, stands on a wooded hill with views over Exmoor and the Bristol Channel. It has sub-tropical terraced and woodland gardens and is home to the national collection of strawberry trees and England's oldest lemon tree.

There has been a castle here since Norman times and in 1617 a manor house was added to the site. It was redesigned by Anthony Salvin in the nineteenth century. The castle has had a relatively peaceful history, though it was besieged by Parliamentarian troops for six months during the Civil War.

Many supernatural events have taken place in and around the castle. The shop, which was originally part of the seventeenth-century stable block, is haunted by a man dressed in green. Stock falls over inexplicably there, doors open and close, and unopened boxes of stock have been ruined by a sticky brown gunge which somehow gets inside them.

The former servants' hall also has an eerie reputation. A alarm engineer working there recently claimed to feel a strange presence and flatly refused to stay there by himself, even though it was only a five-minute job. On another occasion a night watchman was having a short break in the servants' hall when he heard footsteps coming from the room above. Thinking someone had broken in, he went up to the room with his dog, Pardoe, only to find that no one was there. As for Pardoe, he raised his hackles and would not enter the room at all.

One of the strangest things ever to be seen at the house appeared in the modern 'blue kitchen', which was formerly the butler's pantry and silver-cleaning rooms. A young lad on work experience was left on his own to mop the floor there but fled after seeing a naked foot materialize out of thin air! Apparently it was almost transparent but looked as though it was covered in a white powder.

The most haunted room in the house, however, is the Leather Gallery, so called because of the leather hangings which depict the story of Antony and Cleopatra. Male voices have been heard there at night on several occasions, together with footsteps and banging doors. Workmen in the area have felt so uneasy and sick that they have left the job part way through. A cleaner was polishing the floorboards there one morning with an electric polishing machine when the room turned very cold and she saw the shadowy figure of a man in old-fashioned military uniform standing in the doorway to the corridor. She was frightened, but the figure was cutting off her escape route, so she decided that the noise from the polishing machine would scare off any ghost and carried on working! Within about 30 seconds the temperature of the room had returned to normal and the figure had disappeared. A medium who once visited the house said that the ghost was a Royalist soldier called Richard who had apparently died in the castle grounds from a puncture wound above his right eye.

A tall distinguished looking gentleman in grey has also been seen leaving the Leather Gallery and walking into the King Charles room and a lady in grey has been seen on the oak staircase.

Dunster Castle, Mill Lane, Dunster, Minehead, Somerset, TA24 6SL; Tel: (01643) 821314 (general), (01643) 823004 (info line), (01643) 821626 (shop), Fax: (01643) 823000; E-mail: dunstercastle@nationaltrust.org.uk; Website; www.nationaltrust.org.uk. Open daily apart from 25 and 26 December. Evening ghost tours are available. Pre-booking is recommended.

The Farringford Hotel

Farringford House is an eighteenth-century house set in 33 acres of parkland near Freshwater on the Isle of Wight, with views towards the Solent and Afton Downs. Now a hotel, it was the home of Victorian Poet Laureate Alfred, Lord Tennyson (1809–92), for nearly 40 years.

Lord Tennyson's poetry was widely praised, but his life was plagued by financial instability and he was engaged for 14 years before he was finally able to marry Emily Sellwood in 1850. He moved to the Isle of Wight from Twickenham in 1853.

Emily Tennyson loved Farringford so much that she has never left. She has been seen walking on the lawn and is said to haunt the hotel bedroom that was the former nursery, looking after children who stay at the hotel. The sound of a rocking cradle has been heard there on several occasions.

As for the poet himself, he has been seen smoking a pipe in a chair in the library, where he wrote many of his most famous works, as well as walking on Tennyson Down, the nearby hill named after him. In order to get to the downs he had a special bridge built from his back garden, because the front lawns of his house were often filled with sightseers hoping for a glimpse of him. It is still there today.

The ghost of a horse-drawn carriage has also been seen in the grounds and on the road outside Farringford.

The Farringford Hotel, Bedbury Lane, Freshwater Bay, Isle of Wight, PO40 9PE;
Tel: (01983) 752500; Website: www.farringford.co.uk

The George Hotel

The George Hotel in the heart of Crawley is a former coaching inn which dates back to 1615. Though it retains its traditional features, it is now a modern hotel with facilities for conferences, seminars, weddings and other functions. It offers traditional food in the 1615 restaurant and a selection of bar meals in the George bar, which is a favourite haunt of both locals and guests.

An ancient gallows sign stands on the high street outside the hotel door, but as far as is known the hotel is not haunted by a convicted criminal, but by a night watchman. At one time the hotel was being plagued by a thief and staff laid a trap to catch him by leaving out poisoned wine for him to drink. However, the night watchman drank it and died as a result. After that the hotel had no more trouble with articles going missing, but no one seems to know whether that was because the night watchman was the thief or because the real thief had been frightened off!

Apparently the night watchman did sleep in the broom cupboard when he was supposed to have been on duty, and now the cupboard doors often open by themselves, even when they have been locked. Doors to the bedrooms in the old wing have been known to do the same thing. Perhaps from time to time the night watchman is still doing his rounds.

The George Hotel, High Street, Crawley, Nr Gatwick, West Sussex, RH10 1BS; Tel: (01293) 524215; Website: www.corushotels.com/thegeorge. There is parking for up to 80 cars.

Hastings Castle

Hastings Castle, on West Hill in the town centre, is an eleventh-century earthwork motte and bailey fortress founded by William the Conqueror. Today only the thirteenth-century remains of the East Gatehouse, the curtain wall and the Collegiate Church of St Mary-in-the-Castle are still standing. The rest of the castle was destroyed, along with Hastings harbour, in storms during the thirteenth century. After the destruction of the harbour, Hastings lost its military importance and was reduced to a fishing village. The remains of the castle fell into decay and for centuries the site was used for farming, but during Victorian times it became a tourist attraction and during World War II was used in the training of commandos.

There are many legends about the castle. The most famous ghost is that of Thomas à Becket, who is said to haunt the ruins whenever he is not haunting Canterbury cathedral. He may have once been Dean of the church.

Near the entrance to the 'Whispering Dungeons', so called because prisoners could be overheard by guards standing several yards away, a nun in a brown habit has been seen digging. She has also been seen near the outer wall at the eastern end of the castle and has even been caught on camera by visitors.

The area to the east of the castle was known as the Ladies' Parlour and when tournaments were held there a distinguished lady was always present. Rumour has it that a lady in a shimmering white gown can still be seen there on moonlit nights. The sound of ghostly music, perhaps from the tournaments, has also been heard at the castle. In November 2000 a large crowd watching a firework display on the seafront was surprised to hear the sound of trumpets ringing out from the empty castle.

It is also said that on certain days when the castle is viewed from the sea it is reflected in all its original glory.

A sad story connected with the castle is that of a middle-aged Victorian woman who had an illegitimate child with a local fisherman who then deserted her. Her ghost can been seen from time to time in the castle ruins, dressed in brown and holding a baby in her arms. After a few moments she suddenly walks to the cliff edge and throws herself off.

Hastings Castle, Castle Hill Road, West Hill, Hastings, East Sussex. Open daily. Parking is by the side of the road.

While you are visiting the castle you can experience 'The 1066 Story', a 16-minute sound and light presentation on the history of the castle and the Battle of Hastings.

The Hill House

The Hill House is a friendly bed and breakfast in Ross-on-Wye. Set on a hillside with spectacular views over the Wye Valley, the Black Mountains and the Forest of Dean, it is surrounded by over four acres of private woodland. The Wye Valley Walk and Herefordshire Trail are nearby and supper, a sauna, a bar, open fires, locally sourced organic food and the services of a qualified massage therapist are all available to guests.

The rooms are very individual – the Dryad Suite has a seven-foot four-poster bed and a wood-burning stove, for example – and are haunted by an old gentleman in a frock coat and tricorn hat and a beautiful lady dressed in white. Many guests have written about their experiences with the ghosts in the special visitors' ghost book.

The Hill House, Howle Hill, Ross-on-Wye, Herefordshire, HR9 5ST; Tel: (01989) 562033; E-mail: thehillhouse2000@ hotmail.com; Website: www.thehowlinghill-house.com. Bikes are available for hire.

The Holt Hotel

The Holt Hotel in Oxfordshire is a beautifully refurbished coaching inn dating back to 1475. Its 82 *en-suite* rooms range from singles to four-poster bedrooms with jacuzzi.

The Holt has always been a popular hotel, but the clientèle has not always been the most salubrious. In the seventeenth century the highwayman Claude Duval often frequented the inn and was once so impolite as to murder the landlord and his wife.

Duval was the head of a notorious gang of highwaymen. He had been born in Normandy and come to Britain as a footman to the Duke of Richmond after the Restoration of Charles II in 1660. Prosperity had increased following the Civil War and so had travel. The poor state of the roads, however, restricted coaches to a crawl and they were tempting targets for highwaymen. Duval quickly became wealthy and also gained a reputation for politeness to his victims, especially the ladies. He is said to have danced with a lady passenger in front of her husband and to have returned a silver feeding bottle to a mother when her baby began to cry. When he was finally arrested in January 1670 in London and sentenced to be hanged, many distinguished ladies begged for him to be pardoned. However, the sentence was duly carried out. Now it is said that Duval's ghost has returned to his former base at the Holt Hotel.

The Holt Hotel, Oxford Road, Steeple Aston, Oxfordshire, OX25 5QQ; Tel: (01869) 340259; Fax: (01869) 340865; E-mail: info@holthotel.co.uk; Website: www.holthotel-oxford.co.uk

The New Inn

The New Inn in Pembridge, Herefordshire, is actually one of the oldest in the area. The beautiful fourteenth-century timber-framed building was originally a farmhouse. It stood next to the village's open market and this was probably what led to it becoming an inn, as the farmer would have brewed ale for the merchants. By the seventeenth century it had become a public house and for many years was known as 'the inn without a name' and (paradoxically) 'Cooke's Public House'. For a while the local court was held there and according to tradition the 1461 treaty by which Edward IV ascended the throne was ratified there. It was also used as a prison for a time.

Two ghosts apparently haunt the New Inn. One is a young girl who gazes out of the window and is said to be waiting for her lover to return from battle. She only appears to women. By an intriguing coincidence, the other ghost is a red-coated soldier who is sometimes seen carrying a sword and sometimes beating a drum.

The New Inn, Market Square, Pembridge, Nr Leominster, Herefordshire, HR6 9DZ; Tel: (01636) 388427. A wide range of food is served in the restaurant.

Newquay

Cornwall – a county of mysticism and legend! A wealth of ghosts haunt the crags and moors, whilst the sleepy fishing villages along the coast are home to many a haunting tale of smugglers past.

I spent many summers of my youth in Newquay indulging my passion for surfboarding, a second love after football. Newquay has always been close to my heart, although my one abiding memory is not such a good one, and there is certainly nothing paranormal about it. I was surfing off the beach one day when I fell off my surfboard. Then I committed the cardinal error of turning around to see where it had gone. It found me! And I lost my two front teeth!

More scary still are the ghostly goings on at Trerice Manor, a sixteenth-century manor house near Newquay. When the north wing was restored in the 1980s, workmen reported smelling a whiff of perfume and hearing a swishing sound along the floorboards as if made by crinoline. Since then a Grey Lady has sometimes been seen gliding along the gallery before disappearing down the stone staircase. Could this be related to the suicide of a young servant girl who had been seduced by a former owner, the Lord of Arundell, known as the 'wicked lord'?

Trerice Manor, Kestle Mill, Nr Newquay, Cornwall, TR8 4PG; Tel: (01637) 875404; Fax: (01637) 879300; Website: trerice@nationaltrust.org.uk. Open March–October daily except Saturday. Also features flowering gardens, apple orchard, shop, tearoom, plant sales and museum of the history of the lawnmower.

Nunney

The pretty village of Nunney, near Frome in Somerset, is dominated by the ruins of Nunney Castle, which was built in 1373 in the French style and is surrounded by a small moat popular with local anglers.

During the Civil War the castle was besieged by Parliamentarians and severely damaged by cannon fire. Inside the castle one of the Royalist women was accused of being a witch because she had been having an affair with the Parliamentarian village priest. When the Parliamentarians seized the castle, she was thrown into the village stream in the traditional test for witchcraft. When she floated, she was deemed guilty and was put to death by the castle walls. Her spirit is said to wander the village to this day.

The other ghost commonly seen in Nunney is far more modern. He is a man in his thirties who can be found on the A361 between Nunney and Frome dressed in a sports jacket and flannel trousers and hitching a lift to Critchill. Several drivers have stopped to pick him up only to find that he has vanished into thin air – sometimes after getting into the car!

Nunney Castle, Nunney, Nr Frome, Somerset; Website: www.english-heritage.org.uk. Open daily.

Okehampton Castle

Okehampton Castle, the largest in Devon, is a stone motte and bailey fortress near the northern edge of Dartmoor. Founded by Baldwin de Brionne, Sheriff of Devon, in the eleventh century, it was abandoned in 1539 after its then owner, the Marquis of Exeter, was found guilty of conspiracy and executed by Henry VIII. Now it is a ruin.

Legend has it that the castle is haunted by the ghost of Lady Howard, who rides in a carriage made from the bones of the four husbands she murdered. It is driven between Okehampton Park and her old home in Tavistock by a headless coachman and always accompanied by the barking skeletal dog, although some versions of the story say that it is Lady Howard herself who turns into the dog.

As punishment for her sins, each night Lady Howard has to pick a single blade of grass from the castle grounds and return it safely to Tavistock. Once every blade has been taken, the world will come to an end.

The real Lady Howard (1596–1671) did have four husbands who all died before her, but she is unlikely to have murdered them. She was a member of the family that owned Okehampton Castle.

Skeletal carriages aside, strange events have been reported at the castle. A visitor has photographed a strange ill-defined shape at a window at the top of the keep and there have been sightings of a mysterious large dog in the grounds.

Okehampton Castle, Okehampton, Devon, EX20 1JB; Tel: (01837) 52844; Website: www.english-heritage.org.uk. Open daily, April–September.

The castle is south of the town centre, off Castle Lane. There is a car park, woodland walks and picnic spots.

DEREK'S TIP

Remain open-minded. Sometimes people can be too logical and if the full manifestation of a spirit person were to come up and shake them by the hand, they still would not believe in the existence of a world beyond.

Pevensey Castle

Pevensey Castle, strategically situated on the south coast, was originally built by the Romans as a fortress around AD 290. William the Conqueror landed at Pevensey and rested at the fort before moving down the coast for the Battle of Hastings *(see page 121)*. During the Middle Ages the castle itself saw many battles and during the Second World War it was renovated in preparation for the expected invasion of Britain. Today much of the Roman fort remains, together, somewhat incongruously, with World War II pillboxes and gun emplacements. Not surprisingly the castle retains a military air and according to legend ghostly armies still fight here too. They have rarely been seen, but the sounds of battle are often said to ring out across the coast.

The castle is also haunted by 'the Pale Lady'. She is said to be Lady Joan Pelham, who lived at the castle at the end of the fourteenth century. Her husband, Sir John, went off to fight in support of Bolinbroke's claim to the throne, leaving his wife at the castle. Eventually it was besieged and overrun by the forces of Richard II. Lady Joan's ghost now walks the outer walls at dusk, looking in vain for help from her husband.

Pevensey Castle, High Street, Pevensey, East Sussex, BN24 5LE; Tel: (01323) 762604. Open daily April–September; weekends only October–March. Closed 24–26 December and 1 January.

The Royal Victoria Country Park

The Royal Victoria Country Park comprises 200 acres of woods and parkland overlooking Southampton Water. It is a haven for many different kinds of wildlife and 118 bird species have been recorded there. Football and cricket matches, bus and caravan rallies, craft fairs and dog shows have all been held in the park and it welcomes around 360,000 visitors each year.

The park was once the grounds of the Royal Victoria Hospital, which became the country's main military hospital after it opened in 1863. Although architecturally very grand, it was not practical and the design was criticized by Florence Nightingale. Nevertheless, thousands of patients were treated there, particularly during the First World War. However, the high cost of running the building eventually led to its closure in 1958. In June 1963 it was damaged by a fire, which was probably arson, and most of the building was demolished three years later.

The site of the former hospital is haunted by a lady in a grey crinoline dress. She is said to be the ghost of a young Victorian nurse who gave her soldier boyfriend a fatal overdose by mistake. When he died, she climbed the chapel tower and jumped to her death. Afterwards, her appearance in the hospital was considered to be a sign that someone would die the next morning.

The Royal Victoria Country Park, Netley, Southampton, Hampshire, SO31 5GA; Tel: 023 8045 5157; Fax: 023 8045 2451

Theatre Royal Winchester

Theatrical tradition holds that ghostly sightings, rather than being a sign of malevolent spirits, are a sign of good fortune. All of which is good news for anyone attending Theatre Royal Winchester, where there have been a number of sightings throughout the theatre's rich history.

Theatre Royal Winchester is believed to have at least two ghosts, although no sightings were reported from the time of its refurbishment and subsequent reopening in 2001 until a psychic investigation in 2005.

One of the ghosts is believed to be that of John Simpkins who, with his brother James, converted the Market Hotel into the Theatre Royal in 1913. The cartouche on the proscenium arch over the stage originally bore the initials 'JS'. The story goes that John would have preferred the initials 'J&JS' to be engraved. James promised his brother that the omission would be corrected, but he never kept his word. John died and his ghost is reputed to return from time to time to check whether his brother ever changed the initials.

Before the theatre's latest refurbishment, John's apparition used to emerge from the small dressing-room he once used as his office. The ghost would then walk around the circle, stop in one of the boxes and turn and inspect the cartouche before disappearing through a wall.

Another ghost seen at the theatre during World War I was that of a spotlight operator who had left to serve in the army. One night during a performance of Soldiers of the King, one of the cast fainted on stage. When questioned, she claimed to have seen the spotlight operator standing in the wings wearing his uniform even though he was known to be at the front. The next day the boy's mother received a telegram to say that her son had been killed in action.

Other apparitions have also been seen, including a young girl dancing across the stage, and figures have been seen walking through walls. An investigation by the UK Society of Paranormal Investigation in April 2005 detected the presence of several entities. Investigators heard a voice coming from the stage, music playing, footsteps and unexplained noises, and figures were seen in the upper and lower circle and also in the atrium, which was once the backyard of cottages which stood next to the original theatre. The Society called it 'one of the strangest investigations so far' and planned to return to investigate further.

Theatre Royal Winchester, Jewry Street, Winchester, Hampshire, SO23 8SB; Tel. (01962) 840440; E-mail: pressofficer@theatre-royal-winchester.co.uk; Website: www.theatre-royal-winchester.co.uk

Tintagel Castle

Tintagel Castle lies half a mile from the village of Tintagel on the wild and windswept Cornish coast. It was built by Richard, Earl of Cornwall, younger brother of Henry III, between 1230 and 1236 on the site of a Norman castle and even older stronghold known as Din Tagell. It is a place of mystery and romance and is linked to the legends of King Arthur.

The story runs that Arthur was born at Tintagel after the wizard Merlin had disguised King Uther Pendragon as Duke Gorlois of Cornwall and so gained him admittance to the castle. Another legend has the infant Arthur being washed up on the beach by Merlin's cave. This cave is said to be haunted by Merlin himself.

Extensive excavations have been carried out on the site since the 1930s and archaeologists have found that it was inhabited as early as the fifth century. By the mid-fifteenth century, however, the medieval castle was in ruins. Legend has it, though, that once a year it can be seen in all its former glory and that it is inhabited by the ghost of King Arthur.

Tintagel Castle, Tintagel, Cornwall, PL34 0HE; Tel: (01840) 770328; Website: www.english-heritage.org.uk. Open daily, apart from 24–26 December and 1 January.

The Trout Inn

The Trout Inn, a traditional pub and restaurant, is located in a beautiful spot near a weir on the River Thames north of Oxford overlooking Trout Island. Parts of the inn date back over 700 years. It has been featured in Colin Dexter's *Inspector Morse* series of novels and TV dramas, and Colin Dexter himself reopened it after refurbishment in 2002. It is home to peacocks, swans and herons and a ghost, Rosamund the Fair, known as the White Lady.

Rosamund Clifford was a nun who lived in Godstow nunnery, which lies on the opposite bank of Trout Island. King Henry II was in love with her and it is said that he kept her in a secret garden protected by a labyrinth. One of his knights guarded the entrance, holding the end of a silver thread which led through the maze to Rosamund. However, Henry's queen, Eleanor of Aquitaine, was jealous of Rosamund, especially after she had had the king's child. She killed the knight, stole the thread and forced Rosamund to drink from a poisoned chalice. Now the ghost of Rosamund haunts the Trout Inn. Many people claim to have seen her shadowy figure wandering through the gardens.

The Trout Inn, 195 Godstow Road, Lower Wolvercote, Oxford, Oxfordshire, OX2 8PN; Tel: (01865) 302071. Offers traditional British food, a beer garden and braziers for roasting chestnuts in autumn.

Westbury Swimming Pool

The small town of Westbury lies on the western edge of Salisbury Plain. In medieval times it was a part of the wool and cloth industry. It is also noted for leatherwork, glovemaking and the 300-year-old white horse, the oldest of the white horses of Wiltshire, which was once cut in the chalk of Westbury Hill, but has since been covered in concrete and painted white.

The Church Street baths were given to the town by mill owner William Laverton and were opened in 1887, making this the longest-serving swimming pool in the country. The grand Victorian architecture remains to this day. As well as a swimming pool, Westbury baths now offer a health suite with sauna cabin and steam room.

The pool is said to have a resident ghost called George. Over the years he has been seen several times. Some say he is a swimmer who jumped off the pool balcony to his death, while others say he is the ghost of an old boiler stoker. This may be more likely, as he has been seen at the pool edge dressed in overalls.

Westbury Swimming Pool, Church Street, Westbury, Wiltshire, BA13 3BY; Tel: (01373) 822891; Fax: (01373) 859924. Swimming lessons available. Pool available for private hire.

Yeovil Railway Station Buffet

The buffet at Yeovil railway station offers a variety of tasty meals and snacks for passengers travelling through the West Country. It is haunted by the ghost of a woman called Molly. The story runs that she was in service at the beginning of the twentieth century and had an affair with the lord of the manor. When she became pregnant her husband took up a gun and went after the man, but he was apprehended, tried at Dorchester Assizes and hanged for attempted murder. Molly herself committed suicide by throwing herself in front of a train at Yeovil station.

Now every year during the last few weeks of September there are a variety of paranormal phenomena in the station buffet. The room regularly becomes icy cold at 10 o'clock in the morning, electrical equipment switches itself on and off of its own accord and plates are lifted off the shelves or move along the counter and fall gently to the floor, usually without breaking. Several customers have seen this happening and a young man working in the buffet was once hit on the head by a flying plate. The disturbances build up to 10 October and then everything falls quiet again. It is presumed that this is the date of Molly's death.

Since the buffet was rewired in August 2004, the paranormal electrical activity has ceased, but plates are still being moved around whenever Molly makes her annual visit.

The Wagon Train Buffet, Yeovil Junction Station, Stoford, Nr Yeovil, Somerset, BA22 9UU; Tel: (01935) 410420

WALES

Orkney

Wick

Isle of Lewis

Golspie

Elgin

Skye

Loch
Ness

Aberdeen

Fort William

Montrose

Mull

Dundee

SCOTLAND

Glasgow

Edinburgh

Berwick-upon-Tweed

Isle of Man

Hartlepool

Scarborough

Irish Sea

Lancaster

Harrogate

York

Blackpool

Preston

Leeds

Kingston upon Hull

Burnley

Blackburn

Wakefield

Bolton

Barnsley

Doncaster

Rhyl

Manchester

Sheffield

Lincoln

Liverpool

Skegness

Bangor

Chester

Cromer

Stoke-
on-Trent

Derby

Nottingham

The Broads

King's Lyon

Welshpool

Shrewsbury

Burton
upon Trent

Norwich

Great Yarmouth

Leicester

Peterborough

Lowestoft

Aberystwyth

Southwold

Birmingham

Coventry

WALES

Newmarket

Stowmarket

Warwick

Northampton

Ipswich

Stratford-
upon-Avon

Milton Keynes

Felixstowe

Luton

Colchester

Carmarthen

Ebbw Vale

Gloucester

Oxford

St Albans

Epping

Chelmsford

Milford Haven

High Wycombe

Swansea

Swindon

LONDON

Southend-on-Sea

Pontypridd

Reading

Slough

Chatham

Bath

Epsom

Basingstoke

Guildford

Maidstone

Canterbury

Dover

Folkestone

Haywards Heath

Dungeness

Taunton

Yeovil

Eastleigh

Hastings

Brighton

Southampton

Beachy Head

Bude

Lymington

Portsmouth

Exeter

Bridport

Poole

Isle of Wight

Exmouth

Newquay

Bodmin

Torquay

Isle of
Portland

Plymouth

Dartmouth

St Ives

Falmouth

Land's
End

Isles of Scilly

Barmouth

The Baskerville Hall Hotel, Hay-on-Wye

Carew Castle

Ewloe Castle

The Grand Theatre, Swansea

Gwydir Castle

Laugharne

Maesmawr Hall Hotel, Newtown, Powys

The Mason's Arms, Kidwelly

Miskin Manor Country Hotel, Pontyclun

The Museum of Welsh Life, St Fagans

Powis Castle

Prestatyn Promenade

Ruthin Castle Hotel

The Salutation Inn, Pontargothi

Tintern Abbey

Tredegar House, Newport, Gwent

Wales, the land of the Red Dragon. The national symbol of the country has been around since at least the time of the Romans, though no one really knows where it came from.

Wales is a country with a landscape rich in natural wonders and memories of the past. There are caves and cairns, standing stones and Roman remains, ancient ruins of abbeys and castles. Legends abound, such as the one about the mythical giant Idris who is said to dwell on Cader Idris in southern Snowdonia. Anybody spending a night on the peak will supposedly wake up either blind, mad or a poet. How could this country not also be rich in the ghosts of long ago?

I have travelled frequently to Wales both whilst filming LIVINGtv's *Most Haunted* and while appearing in various theatres throughout the country. I have appeared at the Grand Theatre in Swansea *(see page 161)* and although I have not conducted an investigation of the premises, I have been very aware of the shade of a lady who walks the corridors and dressing rooms, especially at night when the audience have taken their leave and the place is as silent as the grave.

Barmouth

Each year I do my best to appear at the Dragon Theatre in Barmouth (and there's a ghost or two there!), though I have yet to visit the town in anything other than wet and windy weather.

I was first introduced to Barmouth by my friends Marie Flavell and her husband, the legendary fast bowler Jack Flavell. Sadly, Jack passed to the world of spirit in 2004, but he was a man amongst men and I will always treasure the time we spent together.

Barmouth is well worth a visit from anybody conducting a paranormal investigation. Apart from its rich history there are plenty of legends and tales of inexplicable events there.

Some of these have been recorded by the well-known English ghost-hunter Elliot O'Donnell. He wrote about fishermen's tales of mysterious lights, or 'death-tokens', which hovered over the boats of those who were doomed to drown within the next few days. This may be fishy or illuminating, depending on your point of view, but be careful if you step off dry land at Barmouth.

The Dragon Theatre, Jubilee Road, Barmouth, Gwynedd; Tel: (01341) 280392

The Baskerville Hall Hotel

Baskerville Hall was built in 1839 by Thomas Mynors Baskerville. Arthur Conan Doyle was a family friend who often came to stay. While he was there he learned of the local legend of the hound of the Baskervilles and used it in a famous case for his fictional detective Sherlock Holmes. However, at the request of his friends he set the book in Devon to ward off tourists. Today the Sherlock Holmes connection is reflected in most rooms of the comfortable hotel.

The hotel is said to be one of the most haunted in Wales. Many ghosts have been seen there, including a gentleman on the grand staircase, a lady in white in the rose garden and a man who walks between the adjoining balconies of rooms 3–7. Orbs of light have also been photographed there.

The Baskerville Hall Hotel, Clyro Court, Hay-on-Wye, Powys, HR3 5LE; Tel: (01497) 820033; Fax: (01497) 820596; E-mail: enquires@baskervillehall.co.uk; Website: www.baskervillehall.co.uk. Paranormal investigation weekends are available.

Carew Castle

The ruins of the tenth-century Carew Castle stand alongside the Daugleddau river in the Pembrokeshire National Park in a designated Site of Special Scientific Interest overlooking a 23-acre millpond. Over half the species of bat in Britain are to be found there. During the 1990s the site was excavated by an archaeological team from Lampeter University, who were able to show that the area had been settled as early as the Roman period. The name Carew could derive from the Welsh for 'fort', caer, and 'small hill', *rhiw*, or from *caerau*, 'forts'.

The castle grounds have a remarkable collection of unusual trees, shrubs and rhododendrons, and close by is the eleventh-century Celtic Cross and the restored Carew tidal mill, the only one of its kind in Wales still intact.

The castle is haunted by three ghosts. One is believed to be the beautiful Princess Nest, the 'Helen of Wales'. Henry I fell in love with her and after she had borne him a son he arranged for her to go back to Wales and marry Gerald de Windsor, an Anglo-Norman baron who was much older than her. Carew was part of her dowry. Later, in 1109, it was captured by the Welsh prince Owain ap Cadwgan who had been overcome by Nest's beauty at a banquet. Gerald is said to have saved his and his children's lives by escaping down a toilet and hiding in the sewers while Nest stayed behind.

Six years later he managed to rescue her, along with two children she had had by Owain, and to kill Owain, but died in battle shortly afterwards. Nest's ghost is said to haunt the ruins, waiting for him to return. Her white figure once appeared in a group photograph of schoolchildren visiting the castle.

Another ghost at Carew is that of Sir Roland Rhys, who lived in the castle in the seventeenth century and, according to legend, was eventually killed by his pet ape. He is said to haunt the north-west tower. The ape itself apparently haunts the battlements.

Carew Castle, Carew, Tenby, Pembrokeshire, SA70 8SL; Tel: (01646) 651782; E-mail: enquiries@carewcastle.com; Website: www.carewcastle.com.

Open daily from Easter to the end of October.

The castle is signposted off the A477 Pembroke to St Clears road. There are two car parks and a picnic site.

Ewloe Castle

Ewloe Castle was built by the Welsh prince Llwelyn ap Gruffudd in 1257 in a wooded hollow to defend Wales against the invading English. It is a traditional Welsh castle with a 'D'-shaped tower. The English seized it in 1277, but the nearby Flint Castle proved of greater military importance and Ewloe Castle was eventually abandoned.

Now the atmospheric ruins stand in Wepre Park, a 160-acre country park between Connah's Quay and Ewloe. The ghost of a nun has been seen walking over the waterfall there. She is said to have been killed by a bomb during the Second World War.

Many strange phenomena have taken place at the castle. Unexplained lights have been seen and the sound of marching men has been heard – possibly former soldiers from the many border wars. One rather bizarre phenomenon is the ghostly singing which echoes around the battlements during thunderstorms.

Ewloe Castle, Ewloe, Deeside, Wrexham; Tel: 029 2082 6185; Fax: 029 2082 6375.

Ewloe Castle is in a remote location. Please visit only in good weather conditions and between 9.30 a.m. and 4 p.m.

The Grand Theatre, Swansea

The Grand Theatre, Swansea, was designed by the architect William Hope of Newcastle and opened by the famous opera singer Dame Adelina Patti in 1897. Since then it has offered a wide range of entertainment. The theatre was extensively refurbished and updated in the 1980s and the Arts Wing, which hosts exhibitions, conferences and smaller-scale performances, was opened in 1999.

The theatre's ghost is the White Lady, a floating figure who sometimes makes her presence known by the smell of violets. No one knows for sure who she is, but there are several possibilities. Some think she is the ghost of a young actress called Jenny who took part in a show at Swansea just before leaving for America – aboard the *Titanic*. Others think she could be Dame Adelina Patti returning to the theatre she loved, while a third possibility is that she is the ghost of a former wardrobe mistress who drowned whilst travelling to Ireland.

The Grand Theatre, Singleton Street, Swansea, SA1 3QJ; Tel: (01792) 475715 (box office). Conference facilities for 20–1,000 people are available at the theatre.

Gwydir Castle

Gwydir Castle, one of the finest Tudor houses in Wales, is situated in the Conwy Valley in the foothills of Snowdonia. It has a Grade I listed 10-acre garden. It was the home of the Wynn family. Katherine Tudor, Mother of Wales and cousin of Elizabeth I, lived here, and later on King Charles I was a guest. One of the main features of the castle is the panelled dining room, dating back to the 1640s, which was purchased by William Randolph Hearst in 1921 and transported to the United States. Hearst never even unpacked it, however, and it was inherited by New York's Metropolitan Museum, which also simply left it in storage. The current owners organized its return to the castle.

The castle is famous for its peacocks and also known for its many ghosts. The most widely reported is that of a young woman said to haunt the north wing and the panelled corridor between the Hall of Meredith and the Great Chamber. In the nineteenth century the room behind the corridor was called the Ghost Room and a woman in white or grey was often seen there and in the adjoining passageway. In recent times she has not been seen, but people have claimed to feel her presence. Some have suddenly felt cold and been touched on the shoulder. The most notable feature of the woman's presence, however, is the smell of putrefaction! Apparently Sir John Wynn (either the first or fifth baronet) seduced a serving maid and when he tired of her, he murdered her and had her body walled up in one of the chimney breasts. The smell of the decomposing body lingered for months.

Sir John himself has been seen on a number of occasions on the spiral staircase leading from the Solar Hall to the Great Chamber.

Other paranormal phenomena at the castle include the sound of children crying when there are no children there and the ghost of a dog roaming the building. The bones of a dog were unearthed in the cellar in 1995.

Gwydir Castle, Llanrwst, North Wales, LL26 0PN; Tel: (01492) 641687; Fax: (01492) 641687; Email: info@gwydircastle.co.uk; Website: www.gwydircastle.co.uk. Open daily March–October.

DEREK'S TIP

It is a good idea to make a rough sketch of the location before starting any investigation. Noting the number and position of rooms will provide you with an easy reference.

Laugharne

Laugharne (pronounced 'Larn') is a pretty town in Carmarthenshire, 'the Garden of Wales', with views over the Taf Estuary. It was the home of Wales' most famous poet, Dylan Thomas. He and his wife Caitlin are buried in the churchyard. The Boat House where he wrote *Under Milk Wood* is now a heritage site dedicated to his life and work.

The town is dominated by the ruins of Laugharne Castle. It was originally a Norman ringwork which was attacked numerous times by the Welsh and was rebuilt by the de Brian family in the thirteenth century. In 1575 it became the property of Sir John Perrot, reputedly one of Henry VIII's illegitimate sons, who transformed it into a fine Tudor mansion. In 1591, however, he was found guilty of high treason and imprisoned in the Tower of London, where he died the following year. In his absence the castle began to be stripped of anything of value. Finally, during the Civil War it fell to the Parliamentarians, who slighted it. The grounds were landscaped in the eighteenth century.

The town is reputedly haunted by a phantom dog called the Gwyllgi, or Dog of Darkness. Like similar dogs in many other parts of the country it is large and black with fiery red eyes. It is said to run from the castle to the town.

Laugharne Castle, Market Street, Laugharne, SA33 4SA; Tel: (01994) 427906. Open daily April–September.

There is a small parking area opposite the castle and a public car park nearby. There is a shop at the castle.

Dylan Thomas Boathouse, Dylan's Walk, Laugharne, SA33 4SD; Tel: (01994) 427420; Fax: (01994) 427420. Open daily.

There is a tea room for snacks and refreshments.

DEREK'S TIP

Research an area to establish the course of ley lines. It has been proven that there is more likelihood of spirit activity in buildings which lie close to or are built upon ley lines.

Maesmawr Hall Hotel

Maesmawr Hall Hotel is situated in the Severn Valley, five miles from the market town of Newtown and a mile from the village of Caersws. It dates back to the sixteenth century and is a fine example of the central chimney timber-framed houses which are characteristic of the area. A large function room has been added at the rear.

A Grey Lady is said to haunt the hotel. She is supposed to sit on the bed in two of the rooms and strokes the occupant's hair and hands.

There are also stories about a very evil man, Robin Drwg, who took the form of a bull and was finally 'laid' by seven parsons and condemned to Llyn Tarw (Bull's Pool). It may be his ghost that is supposed to haunt a small wooded area in the grounds as well as the house.

Maesmawr Hall Hotel, Caersws, Newtown, Powys, SY17 5SF; Tel: (01686) 688255; Fax: (01686) 688410; Website: www.maesmawr.co.uk

The Maesmawr Hall Restaurant, open to the public seven days a week, specializes in freshly cooked food using local produce. *À la carte* and bar menus are available.

The Mason's Arms

Kidwelly, on the River Gwendraeth in South Wales, is a historic coastal town dominated by its Norman castle. English, French and Flemish immigrants were brought into the area to support Norman rule and the town was attacked many times by the Welsh. By the fourteenth century strong defences had been built and the town had become a busy commercial centre. The Mason's Arms dates back to this period and is one of the oldest pubs in Wales. It is a traditional thatched inn with a beer garden. A variety of beers, wines and spirits are served and food is available.

The pub is reputed to be haunted by three ghosts. When a new land-lady moved in recently, she found that all the chairs had been moved round into a circle to welcome her, though no one had been in the room at the time.

The Mason's Arms, 37 Water Street, Kidwelly, SA17 5BX; Tel: (01554) 890298

Miskin Manor Country Hotel

Miskin Manor Country Hotel is a Grade II listed building situated in 22 acres of countryside. It is believed that the name evolved from maes cun, 'lovely plain'. The manor dates back to the tenth century and was rebuilt in 1857 by David Williams, a well-known Welsh bard and philanthropist. It suffered two major fires, the first in 1922 and the second in 1952. During the Second World War it was a nursing home and afterwards was turned into flats before becoming a hotel in 1985.

Staff at the hotel have had many paranormal experiences. The most regular sighting is of a grey mist that floats across the lounge bar from the drawing room at night. At first one of the former night supervisors thought his eyes were playing tricks on him, but one night he invited the security guard in for a coffee and he suddenly shouted, 'What was that?' 'It happens most nights,' the supervisor replied. The security guard never took him up on his invite for coffee again.

One another occasion the same night supervisor was approaching a conference room in the early hours of the morning when he noticed a tall shadow on the door. Believing it to be an intruder, he summoned the security guard. He came quickly and went into the room to investigate. The shadow slid down the door and away from view. There was no sound from the wooden floor, no one came out through the main door and all the fire exit doors were secure, yet a search found no one in the room.

Another evening the bar supervisor drove home at about 11 o'clock. A couple of minutes later the manager on duty carried out his usual check of the premises, which included walking over an old bridge. As he crossed the bridge he felt that someone was walking beside him. The following day the bar supervisor related how she had had the feeling that someone was sitting in the back seat of her car as she had driven over the bridge and that she had been afraid to look in the mirror. The manager and the supervisor had been on different shift patterns and neither had any idea of what other had experienced.

Guests, too, have had strange encounters. One warm night a businessman was lying in bed with the bedclothes pushed down. As he was drifting off to sleep he noticed a figure coming out of the bathroom and moving around the bed until it was level with him. Then it said, 'There is no need for you to worry any longer now you are dead,' and raised the bedclothes up to his chest. Surprisingly, he didn't feel afraid, just relaxed and comfortable. The figure then returned to the bathroom. After a while the guest started to wonder whether it had been a dream. He got out of bed and went to the bathroom to find paper tissues thrown untidily around the room.

Another guest once witnessed a mirror float right across the room. There have also been many sightings of a gentleman dressed in a dark suit looking from the cedar room over the lawn. The ghost of an old gardener has also been seen and the hotel is said to be haunted by a small child who was killed in one of the fires.

Miskin Manor Hotel, Pendoylan Road, Pontyclun, Nr Cowbridge, South Wales, CF72 8ND; Tel: (01443) 224204; Fax: (01443) 237606; Website: www.miskin-manor.co.uk

The Museum of Welsh Life

The Museum of Welsh Life opened in 1948 and has become one of Europe's foremost open-air museums. It stands in the grounds of the magnificent St Fagans Castle, a late sixteenth-century manor house whose ground floor is open to the public. The 100-acre parkland now has over 30 original buildings which have been moved here from various parts of Wales to show how people lived at various times in history. They include a chapel, a school and several workshops where craftsmen demonstrate their skills and sell their products. There are also exhibitions of costumes, daily life and farming implements, and native breeds of livestock can be seen in the fields.

Several ghosts are also on site. At the Battle of St Fagans in 1646, during the Civil War, 8,000 Royalist troops were routed and the river ran red with blood. It is said that the sounds of battle and cries of the dying can still be heard.

Visitors to one of the cottages that has come from Rhostryfan in Snowdonia, the eighteenth-century Llainfadyn, have seen and heard ghostly children playing, laughing and crying.

The eighteenth-century Cilewent farmhouse also has a reputation for strange events. Several visitors have felt icy cold there and on several occasions the building's heavy wooden doors have been locked from the inside during the night. Staff opening the locked wooden trapdoor to the loft recently were surprised to see tiny footprints in the dust on a series of Welsh wooden chests. They clearly passed from one side of the stone wall to another. Neither visitors nor children have access to this part of the building.

The castle and one of the houses are also haunted by a shadowy figure said to be the ghost of the first curator, Dr Peate.

The Museum of Welsh Life, St Fagans, Cardiff, CF5 6XB; Tel: 029 2057 3500. Open daily.

DEREK'S TIP

Don't forget that residual energy does not exist only in the fabric of a building, but does so in the ground upon which that building has been erected. Therefore do not dismiss as rubbish a story of spirit activity with no relevance to the present building's past. The spirits who visit may well belong to an earlier age and a previous construction.

Powis Castle

Powis Castle is a thirteenth-century fortress which has been modified by generations of the Herbert and Clive families. It houses a brilliant collection of treasures, including tapestries, sculpture, paintings, furniture and carriages, and the terraced gardens, designed in the seventeenth century, include many rare plants.

Several ghosts have been seen at Powis, including a man in one of the ground-floor rooms, a woman in white in one of the bedrooms and a man on a horse in the grounds. However, the most famous apparition is that of a gentleman who was seen three times in one evening and has never been seen since.

The story runs that an elderly seamstress had been engaged to do some work at the castle and given a small bedroom but not told that it was haunted. One night in her room she was reading her Bible when a gentleman walked in, stopped at a window and looked out. After a while he turned and left, slowly shutting the door behind him. It was only after he had gone that the seamstress realized that he had not made a sound. Realizing he was a ghost, she started to pray. Then the door opened again and she found the same gentleman standing right behind her. Again he turned round and left. Later he returned for the third time. This time the old lady asked him what he wanted. The ghost led her to a small room and told her to take up a floorboard, remove a box that she would find there and send it to the Earl of Powys in London. He promised that if she did so, he would never appear again.

The box was duly sent to the Earl of Powys, who was so delighted to receive it that he invited the old woman to be his guest at the castle for the rest of her life.

Powis Castle, Nr Welshpool, Powys, SY21 8RF; Tel: (01938) 551929; Website: www.nationaltrust.org.uk. Open April–November. There is a shop and restaurant. Special events are held regularly at the castle.

Prestatyn Promenade

Prestatyn is a lovely seaside town with a long promenade. On a warm summer's day strolling along 'the prom' is an ideal way to relax.

However, at twilight the promenade is haunted by a solitary woman in a white dress: the White Lady of Prestatyn. She is a tall figure who walks between the Nova and the Festival Gardens, although she has been seen elsewhere on the promenade. She has also been seen sitting on the sea wall reading a book. It is thought that she could be a ghostly nun reading her Bible.

A few years ago a Rhyl man was walking his dog along the promenade when the White Lady appeared in front of him. His dog immediately started to shiver and whine and he had to pick it up and carry it under his arm. As the woman approached, the dog gave a terrified yelp, jumped out of the man's arms and ran away. The air suddenly became very cold and the man realized that the woman coming towards him was a nun with no face below her wimple. As he froze to the spot with horror, she passed straight through him, feeling like an icy chill. When he turned, he found she had disappeared completely. He later found his dog safe and well, hiding under his car.

Ruthin Castle Hotel

Ruthin Castle, the Red Fort, was built by Edward I in 1277. Its remains are situated in a walled dry moat within 30 acres of landscaped gardens, parkland and woods by the River Clwyd. In 1963 it was transformed into a luxury hotel.

The castle ghost is known as the Grey Lady, as she is dressed from head to foot in grey. There are many stories about her. The most popular is that when the castle was a fortress inhabited by the armies of Edward I, she was the wife of his second in command. Her husband, however, was having an affair with a local woman. When his wife discovered this, she murdered the woman with an axe. Afterwards, she was tried, sentenced and executed at the castle. As a criminal she could not be buried in consecrated ground, so she was buried just outside the castle walls. Her grave is still there, but her ghost can be seen roaming the castle battlements and sometimes the banqueting hall, which was formerly the chapel.

A man in armour wearing only one gauntlet has also been seen at the castle, but nothing is known about him.

Ruthin Castle Hotel, Ruthin, Denbighshire, North Wales, LL15 2NU; Tel: (01824) 702664; Fax: (01824) 705978; E-mail: reception@ruthincastle.co.uk; Website: www.ruthincastle.co.uk

The Salutation Inn

The origins of the Salutation Inn, formerly known as the Penrheol Inn, date back as far as the fourteenth century. Today many of the original features still remain: exposed beams, some thick walls and the flagstone floor.

In the early fifteenth century many battles were fought in and around the area and the inn was used as a makeshift hospital. Two Celtic warriors who died there still haunt the premises and it is believed that Prince Llewellyn himself walks between the stable and the bar. He has actually been seen on three or four occasions, escorted by the two warriors, walking through the front wall of the bar. This was the main entrance of the pub until 1888.

On the upper floor there are the ghosts of two women. One of them is Jane, who died in 1874 and today roams the pub looking for a box of pearls that her husband stole from her. At one time she ran the pub with her husband, but he drank the profits and died aged only 37, leaving many debts. Consequently Jane was evicted by the bailiffs and died shortly afterwards in the workhouse in Carmarthen. The other lady is Lorna, who died in the pub in the mid-1700s. Apparently she was extremely well to do and would never go downstairs to the bar area. She is reputed to be buried in the cellar. The ghost of her husband walks back and forth in the snug, upset because he feels people should not be walking over the place where Lorna is buried. Several people have felt a physical nudge urging them to move on when they have been standing in that particular part of the snug.

Five ostlers also haunt the pub, together with a young lad called Daniel Davies, who worked with the horses when the pub was used by drovers. The ostlers died in a fire in the pub in the early 1800s and Daniel was killed the same day when he was kicked by one of the frightened horses. The ostlers have been seen in the form of orbs of light in the lower restaurant, which was once the stable.

The final spirits haunting the pub are Henry Selwyn Allen, a former landlord, and Sam, his partner, who owned the pub. Sam regularly makes the lampshades move and opens the curtains at night. He has a sense of humour, but if he doesn't like the way something is done in the pub he will make his opinion known. He has his own place at a table in the restaurant and no one else is allowed to sit there. People always know when he is around by the strong smell of pipe tobacco.

Though the Salutation is one of the most haunted pubs in Wales, it is also one of the warmest and friendliest and all 13 spirit 'friends' make it that way.

The Salutation Inn, Pontargothi, Nr Nantgaredig, Carmarthenshire, SA23 7NH; Tel: (01267) 290336. Serves food.

Tintern Abbey

Tintern Abbey was the second Cistercian abbey to be built in Britain and the first in Wales. It was founded on 9 May 1131 by Walter de Clare, Lord of Chepstow. It soon prospered and buildings were added every century until its dissolution in 1536. Within a few years, though, the lead had been stripped from the roof and the stone taken away for local building projects and the abbey had fallen into ruin.

When it became fashionable to travel to wilder parts of the country in the late eighteenth century, Tintern Abbey was visited by many famous people, including J. M. W. Turner and William Wordsworth, who was inspired to write his famous poem 'Tintern Abbey' there.

A number of visitors have seen the ghost of Tintern Abbey, a monk who prays near one of the arches on the west side. The presence of a Saxon soldier has also been felt in the grounds. Apparently he was killed at the abbey whilst fighting in Henry II's army.

There is also a legend about Tintern Abbey: once some young men visiting the abbey decided to employ labourers to dig in the orchard to see if they could find any antiquities. Two human skeletons were uncovered and the men decided to celebrate in the abbey ruins. As they sat down to their feast, joking about what the monks would think, a thunderstorm blew up and mist came down. Then a gleam of light appeared at the entrance to the choir. It grew larger and turned into a mail-clad knight with the visor of his helmet raised. This was 'Strongbow', Gilbert fitz Gilbert de Claire, Earl of Pembroke. As the men watched, petrified, monks and abbots also began to take shape around him. He slowly raised his arm and pointed to the doorway of the abbey with his sword. The men fled and, as they ran, a small whirlwind gathered the remains of their meal from the grass and flung it far and wide.

Tintern Abbey, Tintern Parva, Chepstow, Monmouthshire, NP16 6SE; Tel: (01291) 689251. Open most days. Church services are sometimes held there.

Tredegar House

Tredegar House is one of the best examples of a late seventeenth-century mansion in Britain, with some parts dating back to the early 1500s. Set in a beautiful 90-acre park, it was home to the Morgans, one of the most prominent Welsh families, for over 500 years, until they left until 1951. For a while it became a school, then it was bought by Newport Borough Council and in 1976 a major programme of restoration began. The house is now open to the public and the grounds include a children's playground, jogging trail, woodland walk and boating lake.

Tredegar has the reputation of being one of the most haunted houses in Wales and a ghost dressed in black knee-length trousers, a white shirt with frills down the front, black overcoat and black boots has often been seen in the grounds. Parades of nuns have also been seen walking through the inner courtyard and one of the outbuildings is said to be haunted. In the house itself people have reported strange sounds coming from empty rooms, unexplained footsteps and the ghost of a nun at prayer.

Tredegar House, Newport, Gwent, NP10 8YW; Tel: (01633) 815880; Fax: (01633) 815895; E-mail: tredegar.house@newport.gov.uk. The park and woodland walk are open all year. The house is open for tours from Easter to the end of September, Wednesday–Sunday. The house caters for conferences and is licensed for weddings. Special events are held throughout the year.

SCOTLAND

THE HIGHLANDS AND ISLANDS

Crathes Castle, Banchory

Culloden Moor

Dunrobin Castle, Golspie

Dunvegan Castle, Skye

Eden Court Theatre, Inverness

Eilean Donan Castle, Loch Duich

Ethie Castle, Inverkeilor

Glen Coe

Inverary Castle, Loch Fyne

The Salutation Hotel, Perth

Sandwood Bay, Sutherland

Skaill House, Orkney

Swallow Thainstone House, Inverurie

The Tay Bridge

Scotland is one of my favourite countries. From its craggy peaks to the gentler slopes leading down to the coast, it is breathtaking. It also has a breathtaking past, with stories of enormous feats of courage peppering the pages of history books. It is little wonder that armies quaked in their boots when they faced the prospect of having to fight the 'Ladies from Hell' – those fearsome soldiers of the Queen's Own Highlanders and the Gordon Highlanders!

The Highlands and islands are full of haunting images with macabre stories of the unknown within the castles of old whose pasts recall the memories of battles fought there. It is no faint-hearted ghost hunter who investigates these locations!

Crathes Castle

Crathes Castle in Aberdeenshire is one of the most popular castles in the care of the National Trust for Scotland. It was built in the second half of the sixteenth century by the Burnetts of Leys. Their first home was on an island in the loch of Leys. The old laird died, leaving a wife and an heir, Alexander. He fell in love with a girl called Bertha, a relative of his who had been left in his mother's care for a few months, but when he returned home from a business trip, he found she had died. Standing by her coffin, full of grief, he reached for a nearby goblet of wine, but his mother quickly snatched it from him and flung it out of the window. Horrified, Alexander realized that she had poisoned Bertha.

Several months later Bertha's father arrived to collect her body. As Lady Agnes and Alexander were talking to him, suddenly the room became very cold and Lady Agnes pointed into thin air, shrieked, 'She comes, she comes!' and fell down dead.

To get away from the scene of all this unhappiness, Alexander left his home and built Crathes Castle. However, it is said that every year on the anniversary of Bertha's death, a ghost travels from the site of the old castle to Crathes. No one knows whether it is Bertha or Lady Agnes.

Crathes Castle itself is haunted by a Green Lady. She is most frequently seen crossing one of the rooms carrying a baby. When she reaches the fireplace she disappears. She was apparently a young girl who lived at the castle, had an affair with one of the servants and became pregnant. The servant was immediately dismissed and when the girl and her baby disappeared soon afterwards it was rumoured that she had eloped with him. However, not long after that the haunting began, and in the middle of the nineteenth century, when building work was being carried out at the castle, the skeleton of a woman and a baby were found together under a hearthstone. Today the Green Lady is heard more than seen – which is perhaps just as well, as her appearance is said to herald the death of a member of the Burnett family.

Crathes Castle, Banchory, AB31 3QJ; Tel: (01330) 844525; Fax: (01330) 844797

Garden and grounds open daily all year; castle open daily 1 April–31 October; restaurant open Wednesday–Sunday 10 January–31 March and 1 November–23 December, daily 1 April–31 October.

The walled garden features yew hedges dating from 1702 and many unusual plants. There are six trails in the grounds and two permanent exhibitions in the visitor centre.

Culloden Moor

Culloden Moor, to the east of Inverness, was the scene of the last battle fought on British soil. This took place on 16 April 1746 between the Jacobites who supported Bonnie Prince Charlie's claim to the throne and the government forces loyal to the House of Hanover. This was a dynastic struggle which resulted in a civil war, with all the horrors and complexities which that brings. Its roots were steeped in religion and ideology. There were Scots and English on both sides and there were also Highland clansmen among the 8,000 government troops led by the Duke of Cumberland.

The poorly armed and exhausted Jacobite army, which numbered less than 5,000 men, was defeated in under an hour. This effectively settled the fate of the House of Stuart. Over 1,000 men were killed in the battle and many more were slaughtered as they tried to escape afterwards. They were buried on the bleak moorland. Their graves are marked with stones, some bearing the names of their clan. A giant cairn of stones stands as a memorial to the fallen. Bonnie Prince Charlie himself spent five months on the run in the Highlands before he was able to escape to France.

Legend has it that birds do not sing near the graves of the clans and there have been many strange sightings by people crossing Culloden Moor. One evening a party of men were making their way home across the moor when a huge black bird rose from the ground in front of them, blocking out the evening sky. While all stared in shock and disbelief, the apparition disappeared in front of their eyes. It is said that Lord George Murray, the Jacobite commander, had seen a huge black bird on the eve of battle – a bad omen and harbinger of doom. He called it 'a great scree' and in his heart he knew that the next day would not go well for his exhausted and starving men. The last reported sighting of what is called 'the Great Scree of Culloden' was in July 2005.

Culloden Battlefield and Visitor Centre, Culloden, Inverness, Highland, IV2 5EU; Tel: (01463) 790607; Fax: (01463) 794294; E-mail: culloden@nts.org.uk

Culloden lies six miles east of Inverness off the B9006. Living History presentations are given at the battlefield throughout the summer.

Dunrobin Castle

This fairy-tale castle in the north of Scotland is the seat of the Sutherland family. The oldest part dates back to about 1275 but major additions were made at the end of the fourteenth century by Robert, the sixth Earl, who wanted to offer an impressive home to his bride.

During the Jacobite Rebellion the Sutherland family supported the government, and though Dunrobin was captured by the supporters of Bonnie Prince Charlie in 1746, the Earl escaped and managed to retake his castle.

Dunrobin is haunted by Margaret, the daughter of the fourteenth Earl, who lived in the seventeenth century. She fell in love with someone her father considered highly unsuitable and to prevent her from eloping while he arranged a marriage to another suitor, he locked her up in the attic. However, her maid took pity on her, smuggled a rope in and arranged for her lover to wait at the foot of the wall with horses, ready to elope. Unfortunately, just as Margaret was climbing out of the window her father entered the room. Horrified, she lost her grip and fell to her death. As a result her lover is said to have put a curse on the Earl, while Margaret herself haunts the upper corridors of the castle and can be heard crying for her lost love.

Dunrobin Castle, Nr Golspie, Sutherland, KW10 6SF; Tel: (01408) 633268; Fax: (01408) 633268

Dunvegan Castle

Dunvegan Castle lies on the eastern shore of Loch Dunvegan to the north-west of the Isle of Skye. It is the ancestral home of the MacLeods and is said to be the oldest inhabited castle in Scotland. Parts date back to the ninth century.

There are many historic treasures in the castle, including paintings, furniture, books, weapons and trophies. The most famous is the Fairy Flag of the MacLeods. Legend has it that it was given to the clan by a fairy woman who promised to aid the clan in times of need if they waved it. However, it had to be waved no more than three times in total and at intervals of at least a year and a day. So far the flag has been waved twice, both times in battle, once at Glendale in 1490 and once at Trumpan in 1580, and each time it has brought victory to the clan.

The 27th clan chief, Sir Reginald MacLeod, once took the flag to be analyzed by the South Kensington Museum. It is apparently made of silk woven in Syria or Rhodes and could have been brought back to Scotland from the Crusades.

People have often heard beautiful music in the room where the flag is kept and ghostly bagpipe music has been heard in the south tower of the castle.

Dunvegan Castle, Isle of Skye, IV55 8WF; Tel: (01470) 521206; Fax: (01470) 521205; Website: www.dunvegancastle.com. Open daily except for 25 and 26 December and 1 and 2 January.

Eden Court Theatre

Eden Court Theatre is the premier arts venue in Inverness, hosting a variety of entertainment, including music, theatre and cinema. It stands on the banks of the Ness, near the cathedral, and was built in the 1970s, but incorporates part of the old Bishop's Palace. Major renovations are currently being carried out, including construction of a second theatre, two new cinemas, two educational studios and a new dressing-room block. The Bishop's Palace will also be renovated and will provide meeting rooms and office accommodation. The theatre will re-open in 2007.

The theatre is haunted by a Green Lady, said to be the wife of one of the bishops who hanged herself there.

The ghost of the murdered King Duncan I has also been seen walking along the banks of the Ness near the theatre. It is not known why he prefers this particular spot.

Eden Court, Reay House, Old Edinburgh Road, Inverness, IV3 3HF; Tel: (01463) 239841; Fax: (01463) 713810; Website: www.eden-court.co.uk

Eilean Donan Castle

Eilean Donan Castle stands on the edge of Loch Duich in a spectacular setting. It was built in 1260 as a defence against Viking raids and became a base of the MacKenzie family, who installed the MacRae clan as their protectors and the constables of the castle.

During the Jacobite Rebellion the castle was first a stronghold of government troops, then taken by the Jacobites. In 1719 it was being used as a garrison for Spanish troops and a munitions store when English forces launched a surprise attack with three frigates. The cannon fire set the munitions alight and there was a huge explosion which reduced the castle to ruins. The ghost of a Spanish soldier is said to haunt the castle, but it is not known whether he was killed during that attack or during the nearby Battle of Glenshiel, which took place around the same time.

The castle remained a ruin until it was rebuilt between 1912 and 1932 by Lieutenant Colonel John MacRae-Gilstrap. Today it is one of the most photographed buildings in Scotland and has been used as a location in many films.

Eilean Donan Castle, Dornie, by Kyle of Lochalsh, IV40 8DX; Tel: (01599) 555202; Fax: (01599) 555262; E-mail: info@eileandonancastle.com; Website: www.eileandonancastle.com. Castle and visitor centre open daily April–October; gift shop open all year.

Ethie Castle

Ethie Castle, near Arbroath, is a fourteenth-century sandstone fortress built by the abbot of Arbroath Abbey. It is said to be Scotland's second oldest permanently inhabited castle.

Probably the best-known person to have lived there was David Beaton, abbot of Arbroath. He moved into the castle in 1524, made many improvements to the property and he and his wife raised their seven children there. He sat in the Scottish parliament from 1525 and in 1539 was appointed Archbishop of St Andrews. He negotiated the marriages of King James V with the French court, but despite his services to the crown he was highly unpopular and on 29 May 1546 was murdered by Protestant reformers at St Andrews. After his death it is said that the monks of Arbroath hid their church vessels, plates and vestments away in the walls of the castle. Not long afterwards Beaton's ghost was seen for the first time at Ethie. He is there still, dragging a gouty leg along the corridors. He is usually seen on a narrow staircase leading to a secret doorway in his former bedroom.

The second ghost at Ethie is that of a child whose remains were found in a hidden room, together with a little wooden cart. He can be heard running across the room and pulling the cart along the floor. He may also be responsible for other strange events in the castle. When the current owners moved in, the pendulum of one of their clocks was broken off in the move and the winder key lost. Nevertheless, the hands of the clock have somehow been moved around to get the chimes to work.

The final ghost at Ethie is a grey lady who walks in the walled garden. Her appearance is said to be a sign that the owner of the house is soon going to die.

Ethie Castle, Inverkeilor, by Arbroath, Angus, DD11 5SP; Tel: (01241) 830434; Fax: (01241) 830432; Website: www.ethiecastle.com

DEREK'S TIP

Always thank the spirits after a successful investigation. A little gratitude goes a long way – even in the world beyond.

Glen Coe

Probably the most notorious massacre in Scotland took place on 13 February 1692, when a group of government soldiers led by men from the Campbell clan killed the MacIans, a sept of the MacDonalds, in Glen Coe, Argyll.

In August 1691 King William III had offered a pardon to all the Highland clans who had risen against him if they would take an oath of allegiance before 1 January 1692. Alastair MacIan, twelfth chief of Glen Coe, not only left it to the last minute to take the oath but also went to the wrong place to do so and therefore missed the deadline. The government was delighted at the opportunity to make an example of the clan and sent two companies of soldiers, about 120 men, to Glen Coe, led by Captain Robert Campbell.

Accepting the MacIans' kind offer of hospitality, the soldiers stayed there for several days, but at 5 o'clock in the morning of 13 February, they brutally slaughtered 38 men, women and children of the clan in their beds, including Robert Campbell's niece and her husband. Others died of exposure as they tried to escape across the snowy mountains.

The massacre is said to be re-enacted every year on the anniversary. There have been numerous sightings of it and it has been reported that the screams and cries of the dying ring out across the glen. In Gaelic Glen Coe means 'Valley of Weeping'.

Inverary Castle

Inverary Castle, a squat grey turreted mansion on Loch Fyne, is the seat of the Dukes of Argyll. The original Campbell stronghold was burnt by the Marquis of Montrose in 1644 and the present castle was built by the third Duke in 1744. He also rebuilt the nearby town of Inverary at the same time. The castle was subsequently remodelled first by noted architects William and John Adam and then for the second time after a fire in 1877. It houses collections of paintings, tapestries and weapons, including Rob Roy MacGregor's sporran and dirk handle.

The castle is haunted by the Harper of Inverary. According to one story he was hanged by Montrose's men, but according to another he was killed in a castle siege. Either way he has been seen in several parts of the castle, always wearing the Campbell tartan, and his music has often been heard. He seems to be a friendly ghost, but rarely appears to men for some reason.

The castle was also once the scene of a strange vision. On 10 July 1758 Sir William Bart, a doctor, was walking with a friend and a servant in the grounds of the castle when suddenly they all saw a battle taking place in the sky. A Highland regiment was attacking a fort defended by French troops. They were soon beaten back and withdrew, leaving a large number of dead. Later Sir William learned that on that very day a British force of 15,000 men had attacked the French fort of Ticonderoga in Canada and had been forced to retreat, leaving behind 1,994 dead. The 42nd Regiment Black Watch had lost 300 men.

It is said that before the death of each Duke of Argyll a ghostly galley with three men on board, similar to the ship on the Campbells' coat of arms, is seen moving up the loch and then disappearing inland.

Inverary Castle, Inverary, Argyll, PA32 8XG; Tel: (01499) 302203. Open Saturday–Thursday April–October, daily July and August.

DEREK'S TIP

A thermometer is a must for any serious ghost hunter as it will then be possible to detect subtle fluctuations in the temperature of a room.

The Salutation Hotel

The Salutation Hotel in the centre of the historic city of Perth has been welcoming visitors since 1699 and continues to do so today. The hotel offers modern facilities for conferences and seminars, a banqueting suite for weddings, parties and other special events, a restaurant with traditional Scottish and *à la carte* menus and a bar with a range of beers, wine and spirits, including malt whiskies.

The ghost of Bonnie Prince Charlie himself is said to enjoy the famed hospitality of the hotel. After landing on the Outer Hebridean island of Eriskay in July 1745, he raised his standard at Loch Shiel on 19 August and, after some initial reluctance, several Highland clans joined him in his campaign for the British crown. The Jacobite army marched across Scotland and reached Perth early in September. The prince made the Salutation Hotel his headquarters and the room where he slept is still used as a bedroom. After visiting Scone, where many of his ancestors had been crowned, he moved south to march on London, an ill-fated campaign which eventually came to grief at Culloden *(see page 188)*.

The Salutation Hotel, 34 South Street, Perth, Tayside, PH2 8PH; Tel: (01738) 630066; Fax: (01738) 633598. There is a public car park next to the hotel.

Sandwood Bay

Sandwood Bay is one of the most northerly sandy beaches in Scotland. Backed by huge sand dunes and a loch and flanked by cliffs to the north and Am Buachaille, a magnificent sea stack, to the south, it faces north-west and is a spectacular stretch of coastline.

The bay was said to be a haunt of mermaids until the nineteenth century. It is still reputed to be haunted by the ghost of a sailor who died when a Polish ship went down in the bay. A bearded man wearing sea boots, a sailor's cap and a brass-buttoned tunic has often been seen on the beach.

The nearby Sandwood Loch and ruined Sandwood Cottage are said to be haunted by the ghost of an Australian who used to visit the area. His heavy footsteps can still be heard. The cottage has also been the scene of other strange phenomena. One couple who spent the night there woke to find the ruins shaking and heard the sound of a wild horse stamping on them.

Sandwood Bay, Nr Cape Wrath, Sutherland. The nearest approach by public road is at Blairmore, a few miles north-west of Kinlochbervie. There is a car park there. Go through the gate opposite. The track to Sandwood Bay is four miles long and well signposted.

HAUNTED BRITAIN

Skaill House

Skaill House is a large mansion lying close to the shore not far from Skara Brae on Orkney. It was built on the site of a Pictish burial ground, which may have something to do with the many ghost stories associated with the house. Visitors and residents alike have reported strange experiences, including ghostly footsteps and unseen people sitting down on beds.

According to one story, a man called Ubby constructed a little island in the middle of the nearby Skaill Loch by repeatedly rowing out into the loch and dumping stones overboard. Eventually he died on the island and legend has it that his ghost came to Skaill House and has haunted it ever since.

Though many paranormal phenomena have been reported at the house, there has only been one actual sighting of a ghost there. Early one morning the cleaners were in the courtyard when one of them looked up and saw a woman with a shawl over her head standing at the door to one of the apartments. They assumed that the people staying there were still there and left, thinking that they would clean that apartment later. But the guests had already left and the building had been empty at the time.

Skaill House, Breckness Estate, Sandwick, Orkney, KW16 3LR; Tel: (01856) 841815; Fax: (01856) 841885

Swallow Thainstone House

During my last theatre tour whilst appearing in Aberdeen I stayed at the Swallow Thainstone House hotel. As we arrived at the hotel it was snowing heavily. The old house looked beautiful under its blanket of snow. As we were welcomed in to the hotel and were shown up to our rooms I was psychically aware of the warmth of the atmosphere. I knew nothing of the history of the building, but it was obvious to me that at one time it had been the home of some rather wealthy people.

That night, after the show, I retired to bed, but in the early hours of the morning I was awoken by movement around the bedroom. I could see clairvoyantly that there was the spirit of a young woman dressed in a very old-fashioned riding habit standing by the window of the room looking out over the snow-covered gardens. She stood gazing wistfully out and then started to move back across the room. As she reached the centre she gradually faded from my sight before disappearing completely.

The following morning I was sitting on my own having coffee in the downstairs lounge. The manageress walked in and stopped to have a chat with me. She asked me whether I had sensed anything in the hotel. 'It's haunted, you know, Derek,' she said. She proceeded to tell me the story of a terrible riding accident that had taken place in the grounds. The daughter of the family who once lived there had been out riding when her horse stumbled and fell, crushing her beneath its weight. She passed to spirit in the house as a result of her injuries.

'Ah! So that's who paid me a visit last night,' I said. 'And I suppose that the room I'm staying in was once her bedroom?'

'Well, we just couldn't resist it now, could we?' she replied, laughing.

Swallow Thainstone House, Inverurie, Grampian, AB51 5NT; Tel: (01467) 621643

DEREK'S TIP

Try a spot of scrying. Place yourself in front of a mirror in a dimly lit room. Sit quietly and relax into a state of light meditation. You may well find that your features begin to subtly alter to display the face of a person who was known to inhabit the premises under investigation. Obviously do offer up a prayer of protection before attempting such communication and always ensure that you are not alone but have another investigator with you when you attempt this experiment.

The Tay Bridge

The first railway bridge over the River Tay in Dundee was designed by Thomas Bouch and was officially opened on 26 September 1877. It had taken 6 years to build and 10 million bricks, 2 million rivets, 87,000 cubic feet of timber and 15,000 casks of cement. Queen Victoria crossed it in the summer of 1879 and knighted Thomas Bouch soon afterwards.

Everything went well at first, but on 28 December 1879 there was a storm so fierce that the engineers were worried that the structure would be weakened. They tried to alert the railway authorities to the danger, but it was too late and a train had already started to cross the bridge. It collapsed under the weight and the train plunged into the river. Seventy-nine people were killed.

Speculation is still rife concerning the exact cause of the disaster, but it brought about a countrywide review of bridge safety. Thomas Bouch died shortly afterwards, a broken man. A new, modified Tay Bridge was built parallel to the original bridge, using undamaged girders from the first bridge. It was completed in 1885.

Many people claim to have seen a ghost train at the site of the old bridge on the anniversary of the disaster and to have heard people screaming.

THE LOWLANDS

Baldoon Castle, Dumfries and Galloway

Brodick Castle, Isle of Arran

Comlongon Castle, Dumfries

Dalmarnock Road Bridge, Glasgow

Dryburgh Abbey Country House Hotel, St Boswells

The Globe Inn, Dumfries

Jedburgh Castle Jail and Museum

The Last Drop Tavern, Edinburgh

Melrose Abbey

The Pavilion Theatre, Glasgow

The Royal Mile, Edinburgh

Spedlin's Tower, Dumfries and Galloway

The Theatre Royal, Glasgow

Thirlestane Castle, Lauder

And so to the Lowlands and the gentler Scottish landscape – but there is nothing gentle in the history of this part of the country. From the Ayrshire coast to Glasgow and on to Edinburgh where the Devil is said to have walked, the paranormal investigator will be spoiled for choice as far as locations for a ghost hunt are concerned.

The most fascinating locations that I have investigated in this area of the country have been the extensive vaults which lie beneath the Old Town of Edinburgh. All manner of paranormal activity is to be experienced here – and don't forget that it was in this place that the infamous body snatchers Burke and Hare plied their trade.

Baldoon Castle

Baldoon Castle in Bladnoch, not far from Wigtown, was built in the early sixteenth century. It was owned by the Dunbars of Westfield from 1530 to 1800, but is now a ruin.

In the mid-seventeenth century the castle was owned by Sir David Dunbar. His son and heir was also called David and it was arranged that he would marry Janet, the eldest daughter of Sir James Dalrymple, a local landowner. She was in love with Archibald, third Lord Rutherford, but as he was practically penniless, her parents persuaded her to marry David instead. They were married in the kirk of Old Luce, two miles from Carsecleugh Castle, the home of the Dalrymples.

On the wedding night, however, the servants were alarmed by hideous screaming coming from the bridal chamber. When they finally broke the door down they found the bridegroom lying across the threshold, badly wounded and covered in blood, and Janet, also covered in blood, cowering in a corner. She never recovered her senses and died insane a few weeks later, on 12 September 1669. Her husband survived, but would never talk about what had happened.

There are several theories as to what had taken place. Some people think Janet attacked her bridegroom, while others think that he attacked her and she stabbed him in self-defence. Another theory is that Archibald hid in the room, attacked David and then escaped through the window. According to local legend, the Devil himself did it.

David later married a daughter of the seventh Earl of Eglinton and died in 1682 after falling off his horse. Archibald never married and died in 1685. Sir Walter Scott used the story in his novel *The Bride of Lammermuir*.

Every year on the anniversary of her death Janet's ghost wanders the ruins of the castle, still screaming and covered in blood.

Baldoon Castle, Bladnoch, Nr Wigtown, Wigtownshire, Dumfries and Galloway

Brodick Castle

Brodick Castle stands at the foot of Goatfell mountain, two miles north of Brodick, the main port on the Isle of Arran. The name Brodick comes from the Norse for 'broad bay'. The place on which the castle now stands may have been the site of a Viking fort. Parts of the castle date back to the thirteenth century, though most of the original castle, built by the Stewarts, was destroyed in 1406 by the English. The first Duke of Hamilton was executed by Oliver Cromwell in the mid-seventeenth century and Cromwell placed a garrison of 80 soldiers in the castle. They restored part of it and later, in the nineteenth century, it was extensively renovated.

The older part of the castle is said to be haunted by a Grey Lady. She is said to be the ghost of a Cromwellian servant girl. The captain of the guard had an affair with her and when she was found to be expecting his child, she was dismissed from service at the castle. Her family lived at Corrie, just a few miles from Brodick. When they heard of her plight they disowned their daughter. She drowned herself in the sea at the Wine Port, a red sandstone quay at the entrance to Brodick Castle. Her ghost haunts the lower corridor, kitchen and turnpike stairs which lead to the East Tower and battlements. She has been seen standing over staff scrubbing floors, as if in conversation with them, but the workers never see her.

Another ghost, that of a man, has appeared in the library, and it is said that a white hart is seen in the grounds of the castle whenever the clan chief of the Hamiltons is about to die.

Brodick Castle, Brodick, Isle of Arran, KA27 8HY; Tel: (01770) 302202; Fax: (01770) 302312; E-mail: Website: brodickcastle@nts.org.uk

The castle is open daily April–October. The gardens and country park are open daily all year round. There is a licensed restaurant and souvenir shop and the castle may be hired for weddings and other functions.

DEREK'S TIP

You do not have to limit your investigation to the interior of a building. There are numerous places outdoors where spirit activity has been noted or ghost sightings have been reported. Ancient battlefields or sites where villages and houses once stood are just as likely to render up paranormal activity.

Comlongon Castle

Comlongon Castle dates back to the fifteenth century and stands in over 120 acres of gardens, parkland and woodland just a few minutes from the Scottish–English border. The original tower house is attached to a later mansion, which is now a privately run family hotel renowned as the perfect location for a wedding.

The castle itself dates from the fifteenth century and was built by the Murray family of Cockpool. The tower house is a well-preserved border fortress of pink dressed sandstone. Guests can take a candlelit tour of the medieval keep and Great Hall, which was used as a living and banqueting room. Unusually, the castle has retained its hinged iron gate, or yett, a defensive feature which was placed immediately behind the studded oak door. The borders were a wild place in the past, with endemic feuding, raiding and kidnapping, and in 1606 the Privy Council ordered the destruction of all the yetts there in an effort to bring peace to the area.

Another unusual feature of the castle is the mummified cats which were discovered during a recent excavation of the basement. It is thought that they were sealed up alive when the castle was built in order to protect it from evil spirits. They are now on display in the basement.

The ghost who haunts the castle is said to be Lady Marion Carruthers, who lived in the mid-sixteenth century. She was the daughter of Sir Simon Carruthers Baron of Mouswald Castle, four miles from Comlongon, and on his death she and her sister Janet inherited his estate. Two powerful local families, the Douglases of Drumlanrigh and the Maxwells of Caerlaverock Castle, hoped to get their hands on it, however, and Sir James Douglas had obtained Sir Simon's consent to marry Marion. In order to stake his claim instead, Lord Maxwell took the castle by force and occupied it. The case was settled in James's favour by the Privy Council in 1563, but Marion fled to her uncle, Sir William Murray, at Comlongon Castle and gave him half her dowry in an attempt to avoid the marriage. However, James sued for his 'just inheritance' and again won the case. At that point, on 25 September 1570, Lady Marion threw herself from the lookout tower of Comlongon Castle. Later it was rumoured that this was not suicide, as was first thought, but murder by some of James's men, who had thrown her from the battlements so that their master would gain the estate without having to marry such a reluctant bride.

No grass would grow on the spot where Lady Marion fell and since then there have been many strange phenomena at the castle and the ghostly figure of a young lady has been seen wandering about in tears.

Comlongon Castle, Clarencefield, Dumfries, DG1 4NA; Tel: (01387) 870283; Fax: (01387) 870266; E-mail: reception@comlongon.co.uk; Website: www.comlongon.co.uk

Dalmarnock Road Bridge

Dalmarnock Road Bridge is one of the eight bridges over the River Clyde in central Glasgow. It is the most easterly of the bridges and joins Dalmarnock on the north side of the river and Rutherglen on the south.

Originally there was a ford at Dalmarnock, then in 1821 a timber pay bridge was built. Another timber bridge replaced it in 1848. Dalmarnock had become a district of Glasgow in 1846. The present bridge was built in 1891 by the engineers Crouch and Hogg and was the first bridge over the Clyde to have a flat road surface. It comprises five elegant spans supported by concrete-filled wrought-iron cylinders. It was refurbished in 1997, but many of the original Gothic parapets were retained.

The bridge is haunted by the ghost of a man who committed suicide there. He has been seen by many reliable witnesses, including a tax inspector. He seems to be a solid and normal-looking man about 30 years old with short hair, wearing a navy three-quarter length coat and black trousers. As he stands on the bridge, staring into the Clyde, people have mistaken him for a real person who is about to commit suicide. But then he jumps off the bridge and vanishes into thin air.

Dryburgh Abbey Country House Hotel

Dryburgh Abbey Country House Hotel is situated in 10 acres of grounds on the banks of the Tweed next to the atmospheric ruins of the twelfth-century Dryburgh Abbey. It was built in the mid-nineteenth century on the site of a previous house.

A woman living in the former house in the sixteenth century fell in love with a monk from the abbey – or some say it was a clergyman – and they started an affair. For a while they managed to keep it secret, but then the abbot learned of it and had the monk sentenced to death for breaking his vows. He was hanged in full view of the house. Grief-stricken, the woman threw herself over the bridge into the Tweed and drowned. Her ghost is said to appear on the bridge and sometimes in the hotel as well, especially when renovations are being carried out. She is known as the Grey Lady.

The abbey ruins are reputed to be haunted by many monks, and the sound of plainchant has been heard there on several occasions. Sir Walter Scott and Field Marshal Haig are buried there.

Dryburgh Abbey Country House Hotel, St Boswells, Melrose, TD6 0RQ; Tel: (01835) 822261; Fax: (01835) 823945; E-mail: enquiries@dryburgh.co.uk; Website: www.dryburgh.co.uk

The Globe Inn

The Globe Inn in Dumfries was established in 1610 and is known for its association with Robert Burns, the national poet of Scotland. The first Burns Supper was held there in 1819. Burns called the inn a place where he enjoyed 'many a merry squeeze', and some of these were with a barmaid, Anna Park. She gave birth to a daughter called Elizabeth, but died soon afterwards. Burns never denied that he was the father and he and his wife raised the child as their own. Burns' favourite seat is still in the inn and the poetry that he etched on his bedroom windows with a diamond can still be seen.

Some say that Anna Park can still be seen too. The inn is definitely haunted by an eighteenth-century barmaid, though it is not certain that she is Anna. However, she is very friendly and appears whenever there are changes at the inn or when the bar is full of laughter. She has a sense of mischief and is said to move things around just for fun and to tug at people's sleeves to get their attention.

There have also been sightings of a White Lady in the pub, especially at Burns Suppers.

The Globe Inn, 56 High Street, Dumfries, Dumfries and Galloway, DG1 2JA; Tel: (01387) 252335; Website: www.globeinndumfries.co.uk

Jedburgh Castle Jail and Museum

Jedburgh Castle Jail was built as a Howard reform prison in 1823 on the site of Jethart Castle, which was demolished in 1409 to keep it out of the hands of the English. It is the only one of its kind left in Scotland. Men, women and children were held there, but it was mainly used for debtors. It was notorious for its cruelty and terrible conditions and was finally closed in 1886 after larger prisons were built in Edinburgh and Glasgow and all the prisoners were transferred. The women's and children's cell blocks are now open to the public and part of the building has been converted into a museum of social history featuring exhibitions of nineteenth-century prison life.

Several visitors to the jail have felt that unseen people were there with them. Some have heard footsteps and cell doors banging and seen unusual lights. A team of paranormal investigators from the Glamorgan Paranormal Society investigated the property recently and recorded orbs of light, flashing lights, smoke, people whistling, doors creaking and the sound of something brushing against the cell walls. Most of them heard ghostly footsteps slowly walking along a corridor.

Jedburgh Castle Jail and Museum, Castlegate, Jedburgh, TD8 6QD; Tel: (01835) 86254; Fax: (01835) 864750; E-mail: museums@scotborders.gov.uk; Website: www.scotborders.gov.uk/outabout/museums/3249.html. Open 21 Mar–31 Oct.

The Last Drop Tavern

The Last Drop Tavern is a traditional pub in Edinburgh's Grassmarket, where the city's public hangings used to take place. The name refers both to the last hanging there, in the eighteenth century, and to the drop through which the prisoner fell. The place where the gallows stood, just opposite the pub, is now marked by a St Andrew's Cross in rose-coloured cobblestones and a plaque with the inscription: 'For the Protestant faith, on this spot many martyrs and covenanters died.'

Originally two tenement buildings stood on the site of the present-day pub, but they were demolished and rebuilt in 1929–30, using the original stone. The doorpiece is dated 1634. The use of the old materials may explain the presence of the ghost who haunts the pub – a little girl in medieval clothing. She has often been seen in the cellar and the bar and likes to play tricks on the staff, calling their names when they are alone in the pub.

The Last Drop offers a fine selection of malt whisky as well as traditional food and drink. Rumour has it that the phrase 'one for the road' comes from tradition of giving condemned prisoners their last meal in a pub on the road to the gallows.

The Last Drop Tavern, 74–78 Grassmarket, Edinburgh EH1 2JR; Tel: 0131 225 4851

Melrose Abbey

Melrose Abbey was founded around 1136 by David I and dedicated to the Virgin Mary. It was a Cistercian abbey and became one of the richest in Scotland, with the largest flock of sheep of any of the religious houses in the country – about 15,000 by 1370. The wool was sold as far away as Italy. The abbey was also a centre of learning and politics. It was almost completely demolished by the English in 1385 but was subsequently rebuilt. In the following years, however, it was sacked four times and in 1545 the Earl of Hertford bombarded it with cannon. After that it never regained its previous glory. After the Reformation the monks were not allowed to recruit new members and the community died out in the early 1590s. From 1618 to the nineteenth century part of the nave was used as parish church, but the rest of the abbey was used as a source of building material for the town and cattle and sheep grazed among the ruins.

The heart of Robert the Bruce is buried in the abbey grounds in a leaden casket. He had sponsored the rebuilding of the abbey after an attack by the English in 1322. On 24 June 1998, the anniversary of Bruce's victory over the English at Bannockburn in 1314, the Scottish Secretary of State, Donald Dewar, unveiled a plinth over the place where the heart is now buried.

Melrose Abbey is said to be haunted by several ghosts, including a group of monks. Michael Scott, a man who is supposed to have practised the black arts, is said to haunt his own grave. A strange figure has also been seen sliding along the ground.

Melrose Abbey, Melrose, TD6 9LG; Tel: (01896) 822562. Open daily.

The Pavilion Theatre

Glasgow's Pavilion Theatre of Varieties opened on 29 February 1904 and is still providing variety today. It seats 1,800 in grand style, with a domed ceiling, rococo plasterwork, Louis XV style decoration, mahogany woodwork and a marble mosaic floor.

All the most famous stars of the music hall played at the Pavilion and it is said that some are still there. The comedian Tommy Morgan was a big hit in the mid-twentieth century and when he died in 1961 his ashes were scattered on the roof of the theatre. His ghost is said to wander the upper floor and backstage areas.

A ghostly woman has also been sighted in one of the boxes in the auditorium and a phantom pianist occasionally plays on stage. There may also be a few spectral stagehands about, as most of the theatre staff have had the disconcerting experience of finding items of equipment moved around or even having them disappear from right under their noses!

The Pavilion Theatre, 121 Renfield Street, Glasgow G2 3AX; Tel: 0141 332 1846 (box office); Website: www.paviliontheatre.co.uk

The Royal Mile, Edinburgh

Edinburgh's Royal Mile runs from Edinburgh Castle to the gates of Holyrood House and is one of the oldest parts of the city. Daniel Defoe called the 'Largest, Longest and Finest Street in the World', though it actually consists of several connected streets: Castlehill, Lawnmarket, High Street, Canongate and Abbey Street.

At one end of the Royal Mile the ancient Edinburgh Castle stands proudly on the site of a former volcano, while at the other end Scotland's new parliament building is situated in front of the spectacular Holyrood Park and Salisbury Crags. In between there are numerous historic buildings of interest, including the Free Church of Scotland College and Assembly Halls and St Giles church. Holyrood House itself was built in the early sixteenth century by James IV and is now Queen Elizabeth II's official residence in Scotland.

Legend has it that the Royal Mile is haunted by a death coach. The death coach, *cóiste bodhar*, *coach-a-baur* or hellwain appears in many traditions, especially those of Ireland and the Isle of Man. It may simply come to claim the souls of people who have just died, or it may race through towns and villages at dead of night, picking up unwary souls and carrying them away to hell.

In Edinburgh, the death coach travels along the Royal Mile from Holyrood House to the castle, drawn by a team of black horses. Some say they are headless, while others say they have flashing eyes and breathe fire. According to Edinburgh tradition, if the death coach is sighted, there will be a disaster in the city.

Spedlin's Tower

Spedlin's Tower stands by the River Annan, four miles north-west of Lockerbie. It was built around 1500 and was a stronghold of the Jardines of Applegarth. In the nineteenth century they built a new mansion, Jardine Hall, nearby and the tower fell into decay. It was restored first in the 1960s and then again in 1988–9.

In the 1650s Sir Alexander Jardine imprisoned a miller, Dunty Porteus, for making bad bread, then left shortly afterwards for Edinburgh with the dungeon keys in his pocket. It was some months before anyone remembered the prisoner was there and in the meantime he had died of starvation. When he was found it was discovered that in a desperate attempt to reach the door he had literally torn his hands from the manacles which bound him to the wall – or had possibly even eaten them away. For years afterwards his ghost could be heard screaming with hunger and pain. Finally, in an effort to lay it to rest, the family had a Bible built into the wall of the dungeon. This gradually started to decay and in 1710 was sent to Edinburgh to be rebound. Immediately the screaming broke out again and a series of catastrophes befell the family. Once the Bible was put back into the dungeon, peace was restored.

Some say the ghost moved with the Jardine family to their new mansion in the nineteenth century. Others, however, have heard strange moans in the tower and felt that a mysterious presence was watching them. Some claim to have actually seen a tall white-haired apparition around the site of the dungeon. He looks distraught and has no hands.

According to local tradition, if you poke a stick into the dungeon of Spedlin's Tower it will come back half-chewed.

Spedlin's Tower, Templand, Dumfries and Galloway

The Theatre Royal, Glasgow

The Theatre Royal, Glasgow, first opened in 1867, but two fires swept the building and it had to close while restoration work was carried out. It reopened in September 1895 and since that time has presented a wide variety of drama, dance, comedy, opera and musical theatre. At one time it was used by Scottish Television to record *The One O'Clock Gang* and it is now home to the Scottish Opera and Scottish Ballet companies and is also available for conferences, meetings and seminars.

The theatre is said to be haunted by at least two ghosts. One is Nora, a cleaner who aspired to be an actress but wasn't taken seriously. In despair she threw herself off the upper circle. Now her ghost can be heard moaning and slamming doors.

The second ghost appears in the sub-basement. Tradition has it that he is a fireman who drowned there while on duty in the 1960s. He has also been seen in the orchestra pit.

The Theatre Royal, 282 Hope Street, Glasgow G2 3QA; Tel: 0141 240 1133 (box office); Website: www.theatreroyalglasgow.com.

There is a fully-licensed restaurant and café. Function rooms are available for corporate events.

Thirlestane Castle

Thirlestane Castle, at Lauder, in the Border hills, is one of the oldest castles in Scotland. It was originally a thirteenth-century defensive fort and was rebuilt by the Maitland family in the sixteenth century. At the time of the Civil War they supported King Charles I and the second Earl of Lauderdale was imprisoned for nine years in the Tower of London as a result. On the Restoration of the monarchy in 1660, he became Secretary of State for Scotland and effectively ruled Scotland as a member of King Charles II's Cabal Cabinet (the 'l' of 'cabal' stood for Lauderdale). His ghost is said to haunt the castle and grounds.

Recently it has also been claimed that there is a haunted corridor in the castle. It is said that people who walk down it never return.

Thirlestane Castle, Lauder, Berwickshire, TD2 6RU; Tel: (01578) 722430; Fax: (01578) 722761; E-mail: admin@thirlestanecastle.co.uk; Website: www.thirlestanecastle.co.uk. Open Easter–October.

The castle is situated just off the A68 going into Lauder. There is a tea room, gift shop, picnic area and children's adventure playground and several woodland walks.

NORTHERN IRELAND

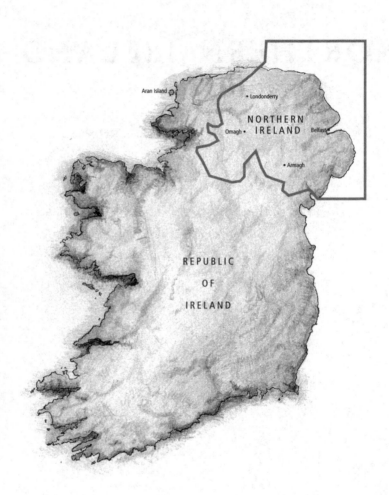

Aran Island

• Londonderry

NORTHERN
IRELAND

Omagh •   Belfast

• Armagh

REPUBLIC

OF

IRELAND

Ballygally Castle Hotel, Co. Antrim

Bonamargy Friary, Co. Antrim

Carrickfergus Castle, Co. Antrim

Dobbin's Inn Hotel, Carrickfergus

The Golden Thread Theatre, Belfast

Grace Neill's pub, Donaghadee

The Grand Opera House, Belfast

Queen Street, Ballymoney

The River Inn, Londonderry

Springhill House, Co. Londonderry

The Workhouse Museum, Londonderry

Ireland! The home of the legend of the banshee – the dreaded harbinger of imminent death!

It is claimed Ireland has fairies instead of ghosts, but of course this is not true. Memories, energies and spirit presences are as evident in Ireland as in any other part of the world.

There are numerous opportunities for paranormal investigation in the province, not least in the walled city of Londonderry, where I have appeared on stage as part of my theatre tour.

Northern Ireland is indeed as much of a land of ghosts as anywhere else in the United Kingdom. Its history is as rich, and whether you are inland or on the coast there is very much more going on than a paranormal investigator's eyes can see.

Ballygally Castle Hotel

Ballygally Castle, overlooking Ballygally Bay, was built in 1625 in the style of a French château by James Shaw, an immigrant from Scotland. The walls are five feet thick and an open stream once ran through the outer hall to provide water in case of siege. The castle was attacked unsuccessfully during the rebellion of 1641. It is now said to be one of the most haunted hotels in Northern Ireland.

The most active ghost is Lady Isobel Shaw, who is known for knocking on doors and then disappearing. Her husband locked her in her room and starved her as a punishment for giving birth to a baby girl rather than the son he had hoped for. She jumped out of the window with her daughter in her arms and fell to her death. It is said that the baby's cries can be heard to this day.

Madame Nixon is another ghost who wanders the hotel corridors and amuses herself by knocking on doors. The sound of her silk dress rustling can often be heard and she has been seen in a room in one of the corner turrets. She lived in the castle in the nineteenth century.

Once two elderly guests booked in at Ballygally Castle Hotel for Christmas. The first night one of the waiters came to their room dressed in medieval costume to invite them to a fancy dress ball. They went down and had a lovely evening dancing with the staff and other guests. The next morning at breakfast they thanked the manageress, but she was horrified. The ball hadn't taken place and wasn't due to do so for another two days…

Ballygally Castle Hotel, 274 Coast Road, Ballygally, Larne, Co. Antrim, BT40 2QZ; Tel: 028 2858 3212

Bonamargy Friary

The ruins of Bonamargy Friary and the surrounding cemetery are situated to the east of Ballycastle in the middle of the town's golf course on the north Antrim coast. The friary, founded in 1485, was damaged in 1584 when local forces set fire to it while attacking the English. After it was repaired the Franciscans occupied it again until they were banished in 1642. Afterwards it fell into decay.

The friary is said to be haunted by the ghost of Julia McQuillan, the Black Nun, who lived there alone after the Franciscans had left. She is renowned mainly because of her Seven Prophecies. There is some dispute about exactly what they were, but they are said to include boats being made of iron and horseless carriages being introduced as a means of transport. The Black Nun is believed to have been murdered on the steps leading to the upper floor of the friary. According to legend she fell on the thirteenth step, and if anyone treads on that step now, bad luck will come to them. Many people believe that she is buried at the entrance of the church under an unusual circular headstone. But she may not be at rest – several people have claimed that a black figure has been seen leaning over the wall or the archway of the upper floor and sometimes it has even thrown stones down!

Bonamargy Friary is on the A2 half a mile east of Ballycastle, by Ballycastle Golf Links, 2 Cushendall Road, Ballycastle, Co. Antrim, BT64 6QP

Carrickfergus Castle

Carrickfergus Castle is a large castle built in 1180 by the Norman John de Courcy after he had overthrown the kings of the north of Ireland. It stands at the head of Belfast Lough and has seen a great deal of military action over the years, being besieged in turn by the Scots, Irish, English and French.

The castle is haunted by a young soldier known as Buttoncap, who lived at the end of the sixteenth century. He definitely seems to have come to a violent end, though there are a couple of variations on how it happened. According to one story, he fell in love with another man's wife and was killed by him *(see Dobbin's Inn Hotel, page 235)*. According to another, he was wrongfully accused of the murder of an officer stationed in the castle and executed.

Carrickfergus Castle, Marine Highway Carrickfergus, Co. Antrim, BT38 7BG; Tel: 028 9335 1273; Fax: 028 9336 5190

Dobbin's Inn Hotel

Dobbin's Inn Hotel is situated in the heart of Carrickfergus, in the shadow of the castle *(see page 234)*. It is one of the oldest inns in Northern Ireland. It began life as a fortified tower house built by Reginald D'Aubin in the thirteenth century and is now a comfortable modern hotel.

At the time of the Plantation of Ulster under King James I, when Scots and other Protestant settlers were 'planted' on estates in Ireland to keep down the unruly natives, the house sheltered Catholics and a priest hole was built so that the priest could escape safely after celebrating Mass. By the seventeenth century the house had become an inn and in the 1660s it was kept by the mayor of Carrickfergus, James Dobbin. In the nineteenth century the building became two town houses and remained that way until it was turned into a hotel in 1946. Early patrons included film star Jack Hawkins and carpet tycoon Cyril Lord.

The ghost haunting the hotel dates from the time of Tyrone's Rebellion, at the end of the sixteenth century. Maude, the wife of Hugh Dobbin, who owned the house at the time, fell in love with a handsome captain of foot stationed at the castle barracks. When her husband returned from the rebellion and found out, he put them both to death. The lovers are still around today, but still apart – the soldier, Buttoncap, haunts the castle and Maude haunts the hotel.

Dobbin's Inn Hotel, 6–8 High Street, Carrickfergus, Co. Antrim, BT38 7AF; Tel: 028 9335 1905; Fax: 028 9335 1905; E-mail: info@dobbinsinnhotel.co.uk; Website: www.dobbinsinnhotel.co.uk

The Paul Jones Lounge Bar, named after the American privateer who engaged his ship with HMS *Drake* off Carrickfergus Castle in 1778, is a popular bar with a nautical theme and has live music on Friday and Saturday evenings.

The De Courcy Restaurant, furnished in the style of the old Dobyn's castle, specializes in traditional Irish fayre.

Guests at the hotel are given automatic membership to leisure facilities at the council centre.

The Golden Thread Theatre

The Golden Thread Theatre, Belfast, presents drama, comedy, dance, opera, musicals and a variety of other live performances. It also runs workshops for children and young people.

The theatre stands on the site of a former mill and its ghost may be connected to the mill in some way. She is a small white-haired old lady who has been seen in the auditorium and prop room and is said to move glasses and bottles around late at night in the Pittsburgh Bar next to the theatre.

The Golden Thread Theatre, Brookfield Business Centre, 333 Crumlin Road, Belfast, Co. Antrim, BT14 7EA; Tel: 028 9035 2333 (general), 028 9074 0122 (box office); Fax: 028 9074 8025

The theatre has a bar and restaurant seating up to 200 people. Rehearsal space with sound and lighting equipment is available for hire.

Grace Neill's

Grace Neill's in Donaghadee is the oldest pub in Ireland. It was built in 1611 and was known at that time as the King's Arms. Donaghadee was once the main port for both the Isle of Man and Portpatrick in Scotland and gunrunners and smugglers would meet in the pub before putting out to sea. To this day its low-beamed ceiling is built from the old ship timbers.

Grace Neill herself was born in 1817. Her husband John was captain of one of the Donaghadee–Portpatrick mail-packet steamers, while Grace owned and ran the pub herself, which was unusual for a woman at the time. She died in 1916, but her ghost is said to haunt the pub. Staff have found books and glasses scattered throughout the bar and electrical equipment has been known to switch itself on and off for no reason. The shadowy figure of a Victorian lady has even been seen on the premises, but Grace usually makes her presence known by the smell of her pipe! A team of psychic researchers investigated the pub a couple of years ago and photographed orbs of light there. It seems that Grace is still welcoming visitors to her pub.

Grace Neill's, 33 High Street, Donaghadee, Co. Down, BT21 0AH; Tel: 028 9188 4595; Fax: 028 9188 4595; E-mail: info@graceneills.com; Website: www.graceneills.com

The pub has an award-winning 80-seater restaurant offering traditional Irish food and many international dishes. There is live music on Friday and Saturday nights and Sunday afternoons.

DEREK'S TIP

Remember, not all spirit return is of the human variety. Instances of animal spirits in visitation to a place they have known are well documented.

The Grand Opera House, Belfast

The Grand Opera House, Belfast, first opened on 23 December 1895 and since then has offered a wide variety of entertainment including drama, comedy, opera, musicals and pantomime. During the 1920s and 1930s variety was all the rage and some of the finest performers of the day appeared at the Grand Opera House, including Gracie Fields, who was given a wonderful reception. During the Second World War, the Grand Opera House became a repertory theatre and to celebrate victory at the end of the war the Savoy Players gave gala performances for General Eisenhower and Field Marshall Montgomery. During the 1950s the Grand Opera House was increasingly used as a cinema. It fell into decline, but in the 1970s, following a campaign by the Ulster Architectural Heritage Society, it was listed and soon afterwards the Arts Council of Northern Ireland funded its restoration.

Today the Grand Opera House is thriving and is being expanded and refurbished. An L-shaped site is being developed in the surrounding area which will include an education suite, including a 150-seat studio theatre, new foyers, bars, a café, function rooms and improved backstage facilities, including dressing rooms for 100 people and a band room for 60 musicians. The opera house will therefore be closed from the end of May 2006 until September 2006.

Cast members coming down from dressing rooms on the top floor of the opera house have often seen another face looking in at them as they have passed a round window.

Other members of staff have been spooked by the feeling that someone was behind them when no one was there, especially when crossing the stage. A woman who was alone in the theatre one morning heard something behind her and then looked up to see a figure in a long black robe on the fly floor. When she looked back, it had disappeared.

The Northern Ireland Paranormal Research Association recently investigated the opera house and claimed to have contacted the spirits of Harry and George, who worked there as stage crew in the 1950s, a woman spirit who liked to tidy the place up and the spirit of an electrician.

The Grand Opera House, Great Victoria Street, Belfast BT2 7HR; Tel: (02890) 241919; Fax: (02890) 236842; E-mail: info@goh.co.uk; Website: www.goh.co.uk

Queen Street, Ballymoney

Queen Street in Ballymoney is said to be haunted by the ghost of George 'Bloody' Hutchinson. He was a Justice of the Peace during in the 1790s and became a hate figure for the United Irishmen, a group of Presbyterian merchants and tradesmen who wanted radical reform of the Irish Parliament. Their subversive activity led to them being outlawed in 1794, but they formed a secret army and in 1798 rose up in rebellion. Hutchinson and his men summarily executed several of the rebels and, once the rebellion had failed, he arrested many others as they returned to their homes. In Ballymoney itself the houses of the rebels were set on fire and much of the town was burned to the ground.

Hutchinson became something of a legend in his own lifetime and legends have even grown up about his death. It is said that as he lay dying in 1845, aged over 80, the body of one of his victims, Samuel Bonniton, was being exhumed. As the coffin was carried past Hutchinson's house, the mourners put it down and gave three cheers. This upset Hutchinson so much that he died soon afterwards.

According to another story, however, Hutchinson came to a grim end when he was infested with lice and decided to cure himself by complete immersion in a vat of manure! At his advanced age it was all too much for him and he died during the procedure, either from drowning in the manure or being overcome by the fumes.

Strange events have been reported at his grave and it is said that when the town clock strikes midnight at Halloween if you walk round the grave three times anti-clockwise and then spit, his ghost will rise up from it. However, it is also said that at Halloween Hutchinson's ghost is to be found walking up and down Queen Street with a ball and chain around its ankles. This is also rumoured to happen every Friday the 13th and on the anniversary of his death.

The River Inn

Each year finds me travelling across the Irish Sea to fulfil theatre engagements in Dublin, Belfast and Londonderry. The Waterfront in Belfast is one of my favourite theatres, but I am always glad to travel across country to Londonderry, stopping along the way to visit that marvel of nature, the Giant's Causeway.

Upon reaching Londonderry one of my first ports of call is the River Inn which is located just inside the city walls. This ancient inn still displays part of the original wall, but most importantly, the hospitality is second to none. And to make it even more interesting, there's a ghost! The young woman walks the short corridor from outside the rest rooms towards the front door. Each time I have visited I have been aware of her presence. One day I will spend a little longer there in an attempt to identify the lady. With Londonderry's history she is bound to have a very interesting story to tell! Unless, of course, somebody gets there before me!

The River Inn Lounge Bar, 38 Shipquay Street, Londonderry, Co. Londonderry, BT48 6DW; Tel: 028 7137 1965

Springhill House

Springhill House, overlooking the hills of Sperrin, is a pretty seventeenth-century Plantation home. It was formerly home to ten generations of the Lenox-Conyngham family and today can offer walled gardens, parkland, a fine library, a caravan site, a significant costume collection and Northern Ireland's best-documented ghost.

Past caretakers and curators have reported a variety of paranormal phenomena at the house, including a rocking chair which starts rocking on its own and mysterious footsteps mounting the stairs, crossing the landing and stopping at the door of the old night nursery.

The ghost has been seen on several occasions. She is a tall lady in a black dress with her black hair tied up in a bun. She is believed to be Olivia Irving, the second wife of George Lenox-Conyngham (1752–1816), who died by his own hand – or possibly hers – in the Blue Room after being very depressed for several months.

During World War II American soldiers who were billeted at the house reported loud banging in the night and came to the conclusion that the noise came from a child's cot in the night nursery. They asked for it to be removed to Armagh and the banging stopped for a while. Now it can still be heard at times, not only in the night nursery but also in other parts of the house.

Springhill House, 20 Springhill Road, Moneymore, Magherafelt, Co. Londonderry, BT45 7NQ; Tel: 028 8674 8210; Fax: 028 8674 8210; Website: www.national-trust.org.uk.

Open March–September weekends and Bank Holidays; July–August Monday–Wednesday and Friday–Sunday.

There is an education centre at the house and waymarked paths throughout the grounds. The converted barn may be hired for functions.

DEREK'S TIP

Do not take part in paranormal investigations if you are of a nervous disposition!

The Workhouse Museum, Londonderry

The Workhouse Museum, Londonderry, comprises the central building, dormitories and master's quarters of the town's former workhouse. It was built in the later 1830s and opened on 10 March 1840, with room for 800 inmates. Following the closure of the workhouses in the twentieth century it became a hospital. It is now a museum presenting exhibitions about the town's role in the Battle of the Atlantic during the Second World War and in the Great Famine, when between 1845 and 1849 around 12,000 people a year emigrated from Ireland via the port of Londonderry.

The most famous ghost at the former workhouse is the Blue Guardian. Hers is a tragic story. She was responsible for the welfare of the children at the workhouse and if they broke the rules she would lock them in an isolated cupboard at the top of the house until they learned their lesson. One day she heard that her sister was seriously ill and left the workhouse for several days to take care of her. It was not until she was preparing to return that she remembered that two children were locked in the cupboard. By the time she opened the door they were both dead. She was so overcome with horror at what she had done that she herself died shortly afterwards. Now her ghost haunts the workhouse, wailing with grief and shame. Many people visit the museum these days, but there is still a melancholy air on the upper floors and few people care to linger alone in the corridors.

The Workhouse Museum, 23 Glendermott Road, Waterside, Londonderry BT47; Tel: 028 7132 9183. Open Monday–Saturday. Self-guided tours are available.

INDEX OF PLACES

F

G

H

I

J

K

L

M

N

O

Oliver Cromwell's House at Ely, Cambridgeshire 23
Osterley Park House, Middlesex 49

P

Parade Shopping Centre, the, Shrewsbury 103
Pavilion Theatre, the, Glasgow 220
Pevensey Castle, East Sussex 143
Pontefract Castle, Yorkshire 70
Powis Castle, Powys 172
Prestatyn Promenade 174
Prospect Shopping Centre, the, Hull 72

Q

Queen Street, Ballymoney 242

R

Red Lion Square, London 51
Red Lion, the, Wirksworth 105
River Inn, the, Londonderry 244
Royal Mile, the, Edinburgh 221
Royal Victoria Country Park, the,
    Southampton 144
Ruthin Castle Hotel, Denbighshire 175

S

Salutation Hotel, the, Perth 199
Salutation Inn, the, Pontargothi 176
Sandwood Bay, Sutherland 200
Shakespeare Public House, the, Manchester 73
Shire Hall Gallery, the, Stafford 106
Shrewsbury Museum and Art Gallery 107
Shrewsbury Railway Station 108
Shropshire Union Canal, the 109

Y

Ye Olde Black Boy, Hull 84
Ye Olde Man and Scythe Inn, Bolton 85
Yeovil Railway Station Buffet, Somerset 150